"THE HAM SHANK"

*by*
MARY PATTERSON

Mary Patterson
University of Bradford
ISBN: 1-85143-090-3 (Paperback) 1993

*To Auntie Maggie*

*Who made life in a slum*

*"A thing of beauty and a joy for ever"*

# Introduction

It is now nearly half a century since Mary Patterson sat down to write "The Ham Shank". It is not a lengthy work but it has a rare literary quality and although it is written as a narrative there can be no doubt in the mind of anyone who reads it that Mary has written about real people and real events in a real place.

As the title of the book indicates, Cockneys do not have, and never did have a monopoly on rhyming slang. The proper name of the district in Mary's story was the Bank. A cramped neighbourhood of hundreds of houses and cottages, most of them built in the late eighteenth and early nineteenth centuries in that part of the city of Leeds which is bounded by the Leeds-Selby railway line and the river Aire and overlooked by Mount St. Mary's Church on Richmond Hill.

In Saxon and Norman times the Bank was an open field, tended by the bondsmen of the Manor of Leeds. Much later it was a place of sheep folds, cottages and gardens. During the Civil Wars the soldiers of the Earl of Newcastle were encamped there, giving Cavalier Hill its name. Many of the inhabitants were clothiers and weavers, some of whom became quite wealthy through trade The Ingram family, for example, who lived in Ingram Hall on the Bank, and the Musgrave family of Musgrave's Fold. Eli Musgrave's tombstone can still be seen outside Mill Hill Congregational Chapel (where Joseph Priestley once served as minister) in City Square, Leeds. Even in the middle of the eighteenth century "Hillhouse Bank", as it was known then, was still rural in appearance, as can be seen in the prospect of Leeds drawn in 1745, from a vantage point on Cavalier Hill.

By the end of the century the Bank was an industrial suburb with foundries, mills, dyehouses and more than five hundred cottages. The houses were mainly of the one up and one down kind, built on the gardens and folds of an earlier time, creating a warren of court and alleyways, often unpaved and totally devoid of sanitation or drainage. Many of the inhabitants were still handloom weavers but their situation became increasingly desperate as the nineteenth century progressed, they could not hope to compete with the power looms and their poverty was highlighted in the Parliamentary committee enquiries of the eighteen thirties. Conditions in the power mills were little better and in their turn they were the subject of Parliamentary investigation into the employment of women and children.

What gave the Bank the character by which it is still remembered was the coming of the Irish. They began to arrive in considerable numbers in the 1820's. Some of the earliest Irish immigrants were the navvies who helped to build the canals and railways. In the 1820's however, the protective tariff on the import of English textiles into Ireland was abolished, an act which practically destroyed the Irish cloth industry. The consequence was that large numbers of Irish weavers sought work in the textile districts of Northern England. In the town of Leeds the main area of Irish settlement was in the east end of the city, around Kirkgate and on the Bank. With the "Great Hunger" in Ireland, which started in 1845, the stream of immigrants became a flood.

The newcomers had to face much bigotry and hostility, not simply because they were poor, with strange accents and seen by English workers as competitors in the labour market, but also because most of them were Roman Catholics. Until the arrival of the Irish there had been few Roman Catholics in the town, which in the eighteenth century had become a stronghold of Methodism. Catholicism had survived in parts of East Yorkshire, especially among some sections of the landed gentry. One such family were the Holdforths. Joseph Holdforth arrived in Leeds in the 1760's and became the proprieter of Banklow Mills, one of the first to be powered by steam. The Holdforth family were to be great benefactors to the Roman Catholic Church from that time on. Joseph Holdforth assisted in the establishment of a mission in 1795, and later in the acquisition of a chapel and schoolhouse in Lady Lane. His son, James Holdforth, was the first Roman Catholic to become mayor of Leeds since the Reformation, although some of the aldermen and councillors objected to his election because of his faith. Perhaps one of the reasons why the Bank became a centre of Irish settlement was because they found a sympathetic employer in James Holdforth.

Because of the immigration from Ireland the Roman Catholic population became substantial, in the 1830's two churches were built, St. Patrick's in York Road and St. Anne's, on the Headrow. Mount St. Mary's church on Richmond Hill, which served the people of the Bank was built between 1854 and 1857. The foundation of this church is a remarkable story in itself, which unfortunately cannot be dealt with here.

There is not space either, to deal with the wretched conditions that obtained throaughout the working class districts of Leeds, the aforementioned lack of proper sanitation and clean water, to say nothing of overcrowding. These conditions contributed to the cholera epidemics of 1832 and 1849, both of which started on the Bank. Despite everything, the Bank was home to thousands of Irish people until it was demolished in the slum clearances of the 1930's. Nor did those conditions break the spirit of the people who lived there. They fought for radical reforms, both for Ireland and for themselves.

Frank O'Donnell was born on the Bank, became the leader of the Labour group on Leeds City Council and Lord Mayor in the 1950's. In the late 1930's he wrote on the passing of the Bank:

".....The other day an imaginative journalist said I was a son of Donegal. He was wrong. I am sure that the sons of Donegal are among the best in the world, but I am not one of them. I was born on `the Bank', by the pleasant water of the Lady Beck on the romantic slopes of Richmond Hill.

`The Bank' in its heyday was mainly Anglo-Irish in its composition. Famine and adventure had drawn men from the County Mayo, or from `the West' as they would call it, to this spot. They first landed at Liverpool and those who came on to Leeds came inland with few belongings and little money to lodge with relatives or friends until such times as they found a house of their own.

`The Bank' had a bad reputation in those days. Policemen for some reason or other always walked in pairs and chased us for playing football `from lamp to lamp'. At weekends when somebody grown up got drunk there was always a fight or two and the more law-abiding citizens closed their doors and bolted the shutters of their windows and stood siege. Our good parents warned us never to stand and watch fights but I am afraid their advice fell on stony ground.

`The Bank' was a great place for all that. Hospitality was everywhere. In confinement or sickness neighbour helped neighbour and troubles were made lighter by kindness. There were saints on the Bank too, Yes, saints, not your smug self satisfied imitations but humble, gentle, wise men and women equal to the salt of the earth. There was humour too, and a kind of pride unknown to the solemn and portentous. But all these are gone now. The old people mostly are dead. The young men have grown up and are dispersed.

If any son of the `The Bank' should read these lines let him visit the old spot once more but never lament its passing for it was never good enough for its people".

Mary's own family were among those who made their way from County Mayo. From near the town of Ballina. Many other families were from the parishes in and around the town of Roscrea which is in North Tipperary. The memory of all them, but especially of her Auntie Maggie, is preserved in this little book.

Danny Kennally.

Mount St. Mary's History Group

(十)

# Chapter I

To the small brown haired girl who played contentedly with her dolls, or romped with the other children on the pavements of the streets and yards of their neighbourhood, came no thoughts of the far away times when she would be "Aunty Maggie", to so many people. Her life was bound up, as it always would be, in the simple intimate things of life. The square stone flagged kitchen with its rag rugs. The shining fireplace, heaped with blazing coals even in the hot summer days, for were not all the meals cooked there? and as her tall sweet faced mother remarked, the men must have their hot meals, with plenty of meat and soups, as the work went on even in the cruel heat of the summer days.

Little Maggie, of the nut brown curls and the grave grey eyes, toddling after her brother John, the flaxen haired favourite of their mother, running to meet the tomboy sister Kate, who, with the flashing black eyes and black plaits would romp and race with all the children, making them scream with laughter at her pranks, or keep them enthralled as she told them tales and sang them the songs they loved to hear, was happy in the cobbled streets so near the beating heart of the great city where the big mills poured forth their smoke, besmirching the air and dimming the sunshine. The joy of sitting at her mothers knee, listening to the tales of that Ireland which seemed to her to be only around the corner. Tales of green mountains rising behind the tiny cabins, of the peat fires burning for years in the open hearths. Of barefoot children running down the mountain roads, their shoes tied round their shoulders, springing happily over the emerald turf until they came to the village church, then decorously putting on their shoes, to clatter down the aisle, and kneel in reverence to hear the Holy Mass. Of potato cakes and oatmeal bread, of midnight raids on the salmon streams which flowed through the bottoms of the gardens, an act of necessary poaching, for did not the fish belong to the Irish, even if the waters they lived in belonged to the English Overlords? Tales of happy times round the open hearths, where the neighbours would gather in the winter evenings, to sing their Irish melodies, and dance to the thin piping of the flute and the "scraping of the fiddle", or gather in the firelight, telling tales of fairies and ghosts, of will o' the wisps and witches. Stirring stories of Erin's Glory, when the kings strode the earth, and every man could call his soul his own. Of conquest and defeat, and ever of rebellion. Amidst the laughter and the shouts, the teasing and the courting, always the love of Ireland came out, steady and sure, deep in the hearts of these simple happy people. In her mother's voice, she could hear the music of that Emerald Isle, in the soft eyes, could see the deep lakes, shadowed with the rugged mountains. Even the shining hearth seemed to vanish, leaving in its place the sweet smelling peat of the eternal fires of Erin.

So into this child's heart there grew a love of Ireland - the place that one day she hoped to see. A fierce protective love - for nothing bad could ever happen in that land of dreaming hills, no wrong could be in a heart that loved a land so fair as Ireland, such was the dream of her child's heart which would perhaps be dimmed by future events, but the love could never be diminished.

It was a crowded, working class neighbourhood, of ugly tiny houses, in streets and yards, and dismal passages, overshadowed by the huge mills and steelworks, which had given them birth. Spotless houses, run by neat and careful housewives, sat cheek by jowl with filthy hovels, run by slatternly women, who lived only for drink and the joys it could bring them. The street in which the Granachan family had settled, was one of the best in the area, the windows neatly curtained and the doorsteps worn with frequent scrubbings. Near by was the shopping centre, low windowed shops, full of wares, sometimes, as, in the case of the furniture stores, spilling them out on to the pavements. Oh the joy of clinging to her mothers's hand, as they went shopping. The odour of new bread and pastry as they passed the open doors of the bakehouses, and stopped to watch the bakers opening their huge ovens, and placing the batches of loaves within, or taking out the crisp brown cakes with their long handled iron shovels. The sight of the pies in the pork shops piled high in the windows, amid steaming dishes of roast pork, and great pieces of udder, cooked and running with gravy in the earthenware plates. The butcher was a tall thin man with an eternally smiling face. Maggie never knew his real name, as he was always called "Skinny Billy" - this because of his extreme slimness, and not because he gave under-weight to his customers. Indeed he was a generous man, and gave full weight and more to them, often putting an extra sausage or piece of liver into the parcel of a needy family. Oh! the embarrassment of Maggie one day, when she was sent there to get some steak, and called him "Mr Skinny!" Looking down at her from his great height, a frown upon his face, he asked her what she meant. Stammering in confusion, the little girl tried her best to explain, that she thought that was his proper name. With a roar of laughter he slapped the meat into the paper, "Ho! Ho! little girl, go home and tell your mother that Skinny Billy is generous today!" Even afterwards he had a tender spot in his heart for the shy little girl who had so politely called him "Mr Skinny".

They were all there, huddled together, the grocers - piled with every household goods that the heart wished for, the sacks of sugar spilling their glistening grains on to the sawdust floor, the cheeses and soaps mingling their smell with the spicy scent of the coffee and the rancid odour of bacon. The inevitable cat snoozing on the counter or stalking the flies in the window. Gone are the thrills and scents of other days, when we walk into our up to date hygienic stores - but sweet are the memories of those old and dusty shops, with the thrill of the sight of their jumbled wares, and their never to be forgotten odour. The furniture shops displayed their bargains on the pavement, the solidly made dressers and chiffoniers, the stalwart kitchen chairs and deal tables standing out in the open inviting inspection. The heavily gilded mirrors tempting a surreptitious glance from the women folk as they passed by, and the general hat tilting and tie fixing of the young men showed that they were not entirely indifferent to their mirrored reflections. The pet shops also were a decided attraction to Maggie, and all the children of the neighbourhood. The tiny birds twittering in their cages, the puppies tumbling about in their boxes, trying to reach the laughing children on the other side of the aggravating glass barrier which separated them. The old parrot, with her ugly face and drab feathers, who swung from her perch in the doorway, screeching at the noisy children running about the doorways, and playing their games in the gutters. How often had the older boys, tossing their pennies in the air, or trying some other mischief, on hearing the old parrot scream "Heck! Heck! there's the Bobbies!" scattered pell mell along the street, only to return with sheepish grins as they realised that it was the voice of the old bird who had given an imaginary alarm.

The horse trams rushing by, the harness creaking and bells ringing, the driver in his high hat, perched high, the whip clenched in his hand, symbol of power and authority. Sometimes, on the waste ground nearby, the fair would arrive,

Rhode's Show in all its glory, and then the fun would mount, the people flocking to see the dancing girls in their tawdry finery, to laugh uproariously at the comedies, shudder in pretended awe at the declaiming ghost in Hamlet, or weep copious tears at the deathbed scenes in "East Lynne". The annual fair which started three miles away, the booths stretching the length of the York road, the garish stalls with their gaudy pottery, the sweet stalls and pie vendors. The shrimps and cockle stalls, the fried fish and chip places, the stalls hung with silks and velvets, laces and moires, a lovely rainbow of stuff, sold at incredibly low prices by the travelling Jews who smiled and flattered, and by dint of much bobbing of black curls and rubbing of hands, wheedled the hesitating onlookers into buying the shining dress lengths and their attendant trimmings.

All this the child saw and tucked away deep in her memory chest. The sights and sounds and, smells of childhood! never again would things be the same. Never again was she to feel the sharp ecstacy that these vivid impressions made on her consciousness.

At first the family had experienced the difficulties of living amongst strangers, mostly hostile to them, when they came to live in this Yorkshire town. As a young girl, Maggie's mother had come from Ireland with her widowed mother, to seek work in the mills. Poverty had driven them from the land o' their birth, for there was not enough work or subsistence in Ireland for the large families living there. As the children grew old enough to earn their own livings, they took the few pounds that they and their parents had scratched from the very earth of their small farmsteads, and emigrated to either England or America. The majority came to England, as they could not afford the fare to America, and there they settled some of them saving up enough to take them even further away from home, a lot of them making their lives in England, bringing up their families, living in the English way, but clinging fervently to their Irish customs, and above all to the Faith of their Fathers.

In those days, the bigotry of the working class English made them cling together. The scoffs and sneers had to be ignored as they set out for Sunday Mass. Bands of young Irish men had to walk together up the main road, the women kept together in the centre, to protect them from the stones and blows that were hailed on them from bands of ignorant colliers, who resented the Irish Papists and stood in gangs to torment them as they went to church on Sundays. Then as the people got used to these strangers in their midst they came to accept them as fellow humans, and stopped bothering them, especially after some of the stalwart young Irishmen had shown that, in a fight, they were as good as, and in many cases, just a bit better than their antagonists.

The widow and her daughter took a small house, and quite soon were busy working in one of the great mills, spending their days in the weaving sheds, so different from the village life in Ireland. Then Uncle Niall arrived, the educated member of the family. He had learned to read and write in their home county of Mayo and a clever fellow he seemed indeed to the others, who had never had the chance of such an education. Then along came the darkbrowed John, who carried the daughter off as his wife and lived with her in another small house next door almost, to her mother.

To either house there was a continual stream of young Irish emigrants, who stayed and enjoyed their hospitality until they found a means of livlihood, which was an easy thing to do for there were plenty jobs for strong healthy young men and women with willing hands and cheerful minds. Then children were born to the young couple, and their lives were full indeed. The eldest child was a son, Edward a solemn studious boy, with large hazel eyes and a keen receptive mind. Mary was the second child, dark skinned and black haired with the red blood coursing through her cheeks. Kate followed, after an interval of ten years, a romping hoydenish child, almost boyish in her ways, then two years later John, with his white hair and fair skin. Last of all came Margaret, with the nut brown curls and the great grey eyes.

Edward kept on at school as a student teacher, when the time came for him to leave his childhood days behind, but soon circumstances sent him to America and there he stayed for the rest of his life. To Maggie, who could not remember this elder brother, he was an ideal, and she loved him in the same way as she loved the country of her dreams. Because her mother loved this absent son, and praised him for his goodness, because of the joyous excitement at home when letters came from America in the sharp clear hand writing of brother Edward, the little girl nursed her love for him and it grew with the passing years.

School days came, happy, happy days! awful, awful days! The sensitive mind of the child shrank from any unkindness, and opened out to the sunshine of kindness. She was quick to learn, and too shy to be naughty so the days of learning passed uneventfully enough. The boisterous sister Kitty took her on escapades that the shrinking Maggie would never have dreamed of. A local station was opened nearby and the children spent hours riding back and forth from the city central station until their pennies and incidentally the patience of the railway attendants

were exhausted, and they were hauled out of the carriages by the exasperated porters, and threatened with dire punishment if they were seen again that day.

Dancing to the barrel organ, or "tingleairy" as the local people called it, was another of Kate's accomplishments and with flying feet and plaits, she would gladden the hearts of the care worn mothers round. Then with any halfpence that may have been given to her, off they would go to the sweet shop for a bag of "hundreds and thousands" - sitting solemnly on the pavements to count them out - one for me - one for you - one for you - and so on in delicious anticipation, tasting the sweets in their imagination as they were scrupulously counted into eager grubby palms.

Then there was the Hoky Poky man, the fore runner of our ice cream man, who came round trundling his barrow shouting "Hoky Poky, penny a lump fetch a pot and I'll give you a lot!" and the children crowded round the cart with their coppers, the less fortunate ones following their luckier friends soliciting a "lick - just a little one."

Then Kate left school and started work in a small tailoring factory, where for a few shillings a week she swept up the clippings and carried heavy bundles of clothing about for the old Jew who owned the place. Then she started work in one of the many woollen mills around, and as she was happy at last in the job, she stayed. Always when she came home from work there was a small tit-bit in her pocket, for the younger sister and brother, who waited eagerly for her home coming.

To the younger children, John and Maggie, the eldest sister Mary was almost a stranger. She was a young lady when they were still too young to really know that the superior being who went out to work and ruled the house with an iron rod when she came in, and who went out at weekends and sometimes in the evenings, always beautifully dressed, was indeed their sister, and not a person from an infinitely higher plane than theirs.

For Mary had grown into a handsome young woman with coal black hair and a brilliant complexion. Her stately bearing and proud manner, her full curves, carefully restricted in the fashionable places by those awful contraptions of steel and whalebone that the females of the day suffered, for the sake of having the fashionable wasp waist of the times. Always preoccupied with her grown up friends, and prospective beaus, she had little time to bestow on her younger sisters and brother, and Maggie a little chilled by the coldness shown her, did not make any loving overtures in the direction of the "Spanish Beauty" the name by which Mary was known by her fellow workers in the mill.

After early Mass on Sundays, which she attended with her mother or Kate, Maggie would play in the street with the other children, time flying by, until the others would stop their play and run to see the "Princess" come home and there they would stand eyes sparkling in admiration as Mary swept up the street on her father's arm, her beautiful black dress sweeping along the pavement, the feathers in her fashionable hat scarcely trembling as she glided along turning her handsome face neither to right nor left, bearing herself with majestic pride which made the other children call her the "Princess" but left a chill round the warm heart of little Maggie, for was not this superb creature her sister,

and yet she passed her by without a glance, disdaining to relax in front of the admiring urchins, even though one of them was the baby of the family.

Then inside the house, all was hurry and bustle, for did not Mary like her dinner to be ready waiting when she arrived home? and it was better for the peace of the family life, if Mary was pleased in all ways. Then in the evenings, after the return from Church, there was fun in the house, for friends of the family would gather there, the bronzed young Irish cousins and their friends, vieing with each other for the favours of Mary and her companions who had all come in for a bite of supper and sometimes a glass of beer for father was an abstemious man and though he liked a glass of "porther" in his own house he would never enter a public house and avoided the Irish Club in the district, because he disapproved of a lot of drink being disposed of by any body and had a horror of drunkenness. "The drink," he was often heard to say "Tis the curse of the Irish" - and indeed it was in many sad cases.

Old Uncle Niall, sitting in his usual place by the fireside, often started some learned or political argument, which often led to the use of big words the meanings of which were queried, "Maggie my darlint" he would say, "Fetch me my dictionary, and we'll settle the argument right away" - and Maggie would run to him with the large black dictionary, and he would open it, pointing along the lines with his empty pipe. Dear old Uncle Niall, with his air of great wisdom, and his never failing humour, the only two books he was ever seen to read, always by his side, the beautiful Missal, and his beloved "Dictionary". Many were the tales he told of the people he had known in Ireland. Of the woman with the lazy husband and even lazier sons, whom she found weeping one day when she returned from the market. On enquiring the reason for their tears, they told her that she must send for the mason at once, as the fireplace was much too near their chairs, and their knees were burning as they sat before the fire. Promising to send for a man to move the fireplace at once, she led them one by one into the back room of the cottage, and made them lie down until the builder had done his work. Then she moved their chairs a foot or so away from the fireplace, and later on called them into the kitchen again, "You can sit down now in comfort", said she, "for the man has been and moved the fireplace back a foot or so". The lazy husband and sons once more took their chairs complimenting their resourceful mother on the speed with which she had had the alteration affected.

Of the two brothers who had a cart given, and argued about who should drive it to market. Blows were exchanged and the two men half killed each other until a neighbour stopped the fight "Shame on ye fighting about who's going to drive the cart to market, when you haven't even got a donkey or a horse to go into the shafts".

Of the man who went a courting at the house of a well to do farmer who had two daughters, the elder almost ugly, the other very pretty. It was arranged that he would wed the pretty one but the farmer wished his eldest child to be first to marry. At the church the bride turned up heavily veiled, and the ceremony over, the groom raised the veil to kiss his bride, and there stood the ugly sister, who had been married to him instead. The heartbroken groom despite the cajoling of the father who offered to double the dowry, disappeared for as he said, "the pigs might die and the land be no profit, but that face would always be there!".

These and hundreds of other stories rolled from the lips of Uncle Niall, told in his soft brogue they had an added charm, and little Maggie would crouch there at his knee begging him to tell them over again, for she never could have her fill of tales from Ireland.

The happy days sped swiftly by, and Maggie saw Kate blossom out from the tomboyish child into a fashionable young woman. Gone were the flying plaits and the rushing feet. The hair was neat and braided, curled into a fringe at the front, and the childish dresses were replaced by the tight waisted, bugle trimmed gowns of the period. Always there was some happy event for Kate to attend. Weddings and balls and wagonette trips to the country, from which she returned, shining eyed and gay, with a bevy of young men at her heels. Happy high spirited Kate with her unfailing kindness to children, her hasty tempers and sudden repentance. Her ardent generosity and her petty meannesses. Everything she did was impulsive and light hearted, a distinct contrast to the more dignified and calculating elder sister. Maggie watched the two of them together, the overbearing Mary jealous for her own glory making sure always that she got the best materials for her dresses. Spending hours at the dressmakers for fittings, coming home in a temper because the same dressmaker had remarked that Kate's figure was the ideal one for the style of the day. Spitefully remarking on the time it took to fasten Kate's corsets, and smirking in a self satisfied way, when, after a strenuous day, Kate fainted because, as Mary truly remarked, her stays had been laced too tightly to make that incredibly small waist.

Patiently and quietly the mother stood in the background, knowing that in the past she had spoiled this handsome elder child, and now must bear the consequences. Pouring out her love on John, who truly was his Mother's "white haired boy". Pampering him, doing everything for him, if he came in tired from play, his mother would place him in the rocking chair, put a shawl around him, and ply him with hot milk. Easy going John submitted to this coddling with sweet temper, even enjoying the fuss made over him. That he grew up into a strong young man, fond of boxing and running, and open air exercise was a thing that his sisters found unaccountable, for the way his mother pampered him should have made him as soft as putty.

Then Mary took a fancy to move into a larger house, and as usual, the protests of the family being of little avail, they found themselves installed in a large house, one of the very few of the neighbourhood possessing a garden, not a very large one, but a garden enclosed by a five feet high brick wall, which gave the house a privacy they had not had in the other street. Although it was not very far from their old house, they were now in a different parish, and John and Margaret, (Maggie to us) had to change schools.

Perhaps the change of house was too much for the youngest sister, the tearing up of those tender roots, where they had clung so happily, setting them down in new and cold soil, spoiled something of their sensitive tendrils, for Maggie was never to know the same happiness in this new house, even though she dwelt in it for forty years.

# Chapter II

The district was jocularly called the "Ham Shank" - as it lay on the banks of the river, and was known in the town records as "the Bank". Hundreds of narrow streets and crowded alleys, smelly passages and dark courts, small houses, tumble down cottages, looming mills and smoky forges completed the picture of the "Ham Shank". To an observer from the wealthy districts no doubt it would have appeared as an appalling slum, but the people who lived there did not notice its cramped houses and shabby appearance, the dirt and squalor of some of its streets, for they had mostly been born and bred in such districts, and the familiar streets looked quite all right to them. The populace was mixed one, hard working families with spotless houses and respectable clothes, ragged, filthy people who came to stay only for a short time, and after they had dodged the rentman and police for as long as they could, folded up their tents in the night and like the arabs silently stole away. There were homely men who cherished their wives and families, living side by side with wifebeaters. Honest men were neighboured to rogues and vagabonds. Truly, the Bank was a morally cosmopolitan place. There, in those days, the police had to patrol the district in pairs and sometimes more after dark, yet a law abiding dweller could wander abroad unmolested, if he had the sense to mind his own business, and simple life went on amidst the undercurrent of murkier pastimes.

The new school that Maggie and John now attended was attached to the parish church of St Mary's, built high upon the hill. It stood up there, the church supreme, commanding a view of almost the whole town, the mean streets stretching far into the distance, almost hidden in the smoke haze from the city chimneys. Not so long before, the hill and the surrounding districts had worn a mantle of green, the great trees spreading their shade for the browsing cattle, the chattering streams running through the lush meadows. From the hill top, it has been said, Oliver Cromwell caught his first glimpse of Kirkstall Abbey, and even now, on an exceptionally clear day, one could see the ruins of the old abbey walls, stately and enduring, past the ugly city that had grown up, child of industry and commerce, covering the once verdant hill and valley with its thrusting, besmirching tentacles, like some loathsome giant octopus. The church itself, had not been built long then, and its austere beauty caught and held one spell-bound with its serene loveliness. It had been founded at great cost and through sheer perseverance by the Oblate Priests of the Immaculate Conception, who had opened a small house at first nearby, which had been lent to them by the Protestant clergy of the neighbouring Church of St Saviours. The people who lived around were irreligious and it seemed almost a miracle that some of them were brought once more within the folds of the Catholic Church. As the Irish settlers arrived, the congregation grew and so the Church had been built. A true story is told of the Parish Priest in charge of the building, who had come to the end of his meagre resources. The contractors refused to put another stone on the building until at least two hundred pounds was put into their hands, as a security on further debts that would have to be contracted. The priest, gathered together his little flock, and they made a novena to St Benedict Joseph Labre, the beggar saint. On the last day of the novena he was pacing outside his church, looking at the skeleton-like scaffolding, something akin to despair in his heart, when he was approached by a stranger, who after a few words about the church, thrust a package into his hands, and strode quickly away. The bewildered priest opened the package and saw a large amount of money; he ran in the direction the stranger had taken, only to find that he had completey vanished. On counting the money they found the sum was exactly the amount that the contractors were demanding. The identity of the stranger was never discovered, nor was he ever seen again in the vicinity, but it was through the miracle of his intervention that the building of the church was recommenced, and its construction finally completed. Later there were schools and a convent built, also a fine presbytery, and then a large orphanage and a college for girls. Like a silent sentinel amongst them all, there on the summit of the hill, was the beautiful church which had begun with so much heartbreak, and produced such wonderful results. Mount St Mary's. There is magic in the name for those who were brought within its loving care. Where ever the flock had to scatter, even to the ends of the earth, there was to them, each and every one, no place to compare with Mount St Mary's.

It was to this church and school then that Maggie and John came when they removed to the new house, and soon they were at home in their new surroundings and they passed the years up to their school leaving age in contentment. There were the concerts given by the school children to celebrate the feast of St Patrick when the girls in their white dresses and emerald sashes and ribbons sang the Irish songs and their parents, proud and happy, came along to applaud them. Maggie could feel the cold chill that overcame her when the great night came, and always felt it vicariously for those other children whom she was destined to watch in the years to come.

Then John went off to work in the mills, and Maggie followed shortly. She tried to work at a rabbit skin factory, but the smell and the work it entailed made her sick and depressed. Then a shoe protector factory opened its doors to the nervous girl, and here she was not happy. Quiet, and deeply sensitive, she was unused to the rough jokes and vulgar talk of the more robust of her workmates, and for the year or two she worked there, never was there any peace or happiness for the timid Maggie. Soon her mother's health broke down, and so the youngest daughter stayed at home to help her mother with the housekeeping. Both Mary and Kate were earning good money in the mills, and were loath to give up their jobs, so on to Maggie fell the onus of sick nursing and housekeeping.

The sound of gaiety went on in the lives of the two elder sisters. They had their balls and parties, and their young men to keep them entertained, and gave little attention to the young sister who looked after their welfare. They helped with the household work when they had finished in the mill, Kate spending more time at home than Mary. Maggie had her girl friends, who had been her school companions, and spent her spare time with them, usually at church services and functions. The social evenings in the church hall, and walks into the more countrified parts of the town consisted of Maggies pleasures. Dances held little appeal for her, as her shyness spoiled all thoughts of pleasure. Her feet felt like weights when she thought of partners claiming her for dances. So, as most shy people do, she took the line of least resistance and avoided dancing altogether.

John was fast becoming an athletic young man. He had made his source of pleasure, amateur boxing, running and weight lifting, and spent most of his evenings training at a local gymnasium, soon to become a well known and popular figure amongst the athletic circles of the city. When Maggie reached the age of eighteen, Mary spent more time at home. Most of the friends she had formerly gone around with had settled down to marriage and the raising of families. The young men who had clustered around, had grown tired of waiting for Mary to make up her mind, and had transferred their affections elsewhere. The only one of her beaus for whom Mary had cared, set out for South Africa years before, to go to a good position, and when he had found conditions to his liking, he sent for Mary to join him. The poor health of the mother made Mary hesitate. She could not bear to go so far away from her parents, and so with breaking heart, she wrote and finished with the man she loved in Africa. Then, since most of her friends were pre-occupied with their husbands and families, Mary was very much alone, and for the first time sought the companionship of the little sister whom she had rarely noticed before. The difference in their ages at that time was a gap that Maggie felt keenly, and as her friends were all of the same age as herself, she was unhappy and embarrassed when Mary came along with her to join in their trips and excursions. The elder sister put a damp cloud on the younger enthusiasms of the other, and so rather than have the enjoyment of her companions spoiled, Maggie made excuses, her home duties and failing health of their mother, and stopped going out with her friends. Oh Maggie! Maggie! if only you had had the courage to speak your mind to Mary, how different might your life have been.

Then John brought home his prospective bride, and the family all fell in love with her sweetness and her beauty. The hair of pure gold and the sea blue eyes. The complexion of roses and cream, so pure, that, even in those days of natural complexions, many were the fights in which John had conquered, as some people found it difficult to believe that Rosie's cheeks were not painted, and had been unwise enough to say so in John's hearing. Soon they were married and took a small house near by, the new wife showing great capabilities in her new office.

Then their first child was born, a son, but their joy was tempered with sorrow, for his feet were twisted, although the doctors said that a cure could be effected, they could foresee the weary years of pain ahead for the little mite, who slept so soundly in his mother's arms. Mary too, found a new joy and occupation with the advent of her new sister, and then the child. Gone was the proud and haughty manner, although the straightness of her carriage never relaxed. Their time from then on was fully occupied, in the ministrations to Edward the baby, and to his brother and sister who were born in quick succession after him.

To Kate, who had always loved babies, even when she was a child herself, the little family was a source of joy and amusement, and gradually her round of gaiety ceased, as, turning her back on all her admirers, she lost herself in the task of looking after the children every spare moment that she had.

This was a period then, when the three sisters were united in a common interest, and the years sped happily by. Rosie brought new sunshine to the house of Granachans, and, despite the frequent heartbreaking journeys to the hospital with her eldest child, a task which was shared mostly by Maggie, as Mary and Kate were still at work in the mills, the unfailing good humour and common sense of the mother made life a very complete thing indeed. There were lean times too, for Maggie's father died, and sorrow came to the house. Then John fell out of work, and the depleted households carried on a struggle to keep their heads above water, and poverty at bay.

Rosie was expecting her fourth child, and John took a desperate chance of making some money to help the household along. He had been an excellent boxer in his day, but after his marriage, had stopped his activities in that direction. However, he met his old trainer, who told him of a chance to fight one of the champion boxers of the day. Lack of training and lack of proper nourishment recently had weakened John's physique, but his spirit made him accept the challenge, and forthwith, he and the trainer set out to Hull, and there the fight was staged. In his condition, John was no match for the champion, but he fought gamely, thinking of the money and what it could do for his loved ones. He was carried off after several rounds, a blow on a vulnerable point, paralysing him down his left side. There he lay, helpless for over two weeks, his wife and her new baby in the opposite bed. Even this could not quench the never failing good humour of Rosie, who laughed and joked with him until he felt much better. The three sisters were kept busy administering to their patients, and tending the little ones, and indeed their time flew by, and they had little chance of repining the pleasures they could have been enjoying elsewhere. Indeed, as Maggie often said afterwards, that though they had their troubles then, those days with Rosie and her babies were the happiest in her life.

Then John got a steady job as a porter at the leading hospital of the city, and things were bright again. They removed to a new and better neighbourhood, but often came back to the old house for visits, and the sisters spent a great deal of their spare time and most of their weekends visiting John, Rosie and their children. It seems though, that good times do not last forever and there was a sorrowful time again. The two middle children contracted measles, and John the youngest boy took pneumonia, and died, followed shortly by his elder sister Maggie. As John had always been a delicate child, the shock was not so great, but Maggie was a healthy sturdy child, and they found it hard to believe that she had succumbed to the disease. The sufferings of the parents were little greater than those of their sisters, for the children had been dearly loved by all.

By this time the eldest child Edward, was able to run around, the steel calipers helping to strengthen his legs and feet. Kitty, the youngest, was a tiny, self-willed little thing, who ran around the house and street seeming too small to walk, so that strangers stopped and stared at her in amazement, as her tiny figure, no bigger than a large sized doll, danced before them on the pavement.

Soon after, as though to make up for the loss of her other two babies, Rosie had her fifth child, a bouncing baby girl, whom she called Mary. This child was a placid solid child, who inherited her mother's rosy cheeks and golden hair. Kitty had a thatch of black hair, but when she started to run about this thatch came off, leaving silky golden hair to follow in its wake. The children were very much alike, but Mary would always be the bigger of the two and as they grew older, although there was a difference of two and a half years in their ages, they were always accepted as twins by people who did not know them very well.

Then, one August day, as Edward was nine, Kitty five and Mary two years old, Maggie and Mary came to visit them. The whole country was in a state of torment, for war had been declared, and England was gathering her strength to fight against the might of Germany. Perturbed, they entered the house to find an optimistic Rosie, "It will all be over for Christmas" she said, as thousands all over the land were assuring each other - "We'll be celebrating the end of the war at Christmas".

But Rosie was never to celebrate the peace that came so late. Within ten days she was dead. Appendicitis carried her off in a few days, and her husband and his sisters could not believe it was true. The horrible nightmare of those days when Rosie was so ill, the days of mourning and the funeral passed like some terrible dream from which there was no awakening. Mary said later "Our hearts were broken when Rosie died, and they have never mended since".

# Chapter III

The motherless children came to live at their grandmother's, under the care of their three aunts, and then John closed up his house, and he too came back to live with them. The grief had to be stifled, and life go on, for there were harder times coming, and people shaped their lives accordingly. Mary and Kate took jobs in war factories, making shells and fuses, and doing men's work. John was kept on at the hospital, as he was needed there to deal with the war casualties who poured in daily, in a never ending stream. The children noticed little difference in their environment, as they were used to their grandmother's house, and accepted the change as children do, too busy with the present to question the past, or probe the future.

To Maggie with the added burden of the three children and her brother to look after, life was very busy indeed. Her mother's health had not improved, and although she was not bedfast, she need patient care and attention. Edward and Kitty were sent to school at Mount St Mary's, as their father had been, before them, and Mary the baby, not yet old enough for school, was a good companion for her Aunty Maggie. Never did the child ask a question that was not answered patiently. The love and patience of Aunty Maggie was a thing the child took for granted, but, when in time, she had children of her own, the greatness of that love and boundless gentleness, took on a new significance.

Memories of other times when there had been another house to live in, and a loved mother to run to, faded from the child's mind, and as she grew old enough to play outdoors, the fact that other children had mothers and she was without one, gave her no sense of loss, rather one of importance, for when people looked on her with pitying eyes and she caught the words "Poor motherless child", she felt no empty grief, for was there not her Aunty Maggie, the hub and centre of her very existence? No hands could have been more tender when bruised knees and hands were dressed, no arms more comforting when tears were falling from a hurt child's eyes, no voice sweeter when singing a lullabye, than were the hands and arms and voice of her beloved Aunty Maggie.

Grandma sat in the corner by the fireplace, never moving all the day, her hair still a beautiful shade of brown, which fell in two long plaits when she let it down to comb it. Then the rippling hair would fall in cascades down to her waist, and little Mary was allowed to brush it, very gently.

When her brother and sister came home from school, the kitchen was full of their chatter, for Kitty had a ceaseless tongue, which got her into severe trouble at school. The irons on her brother's legs never were noticed by Mary, who accepted them as part of him, and indeed never realised he wore them until one happy day, she went into his bedroom and found him throwing them in the air, dancing with joy because he need never wear them again. After fourteen operations, he was cured, and walked, ran and played as other children.

In those dark days of the war, there was much to do for the harrassed housewife. The queuing and scraping, the searching for little extras, all these formed Maggie's day, and often Mary went with her listening wide eyed to the talk of the other women shoppers who were standing in the queues. The jokes about margarine, which they called maggieann, for fun, the mysterious word saccharine, the grumbles over the dark flour, and the horseflesh, that they were sometimes of necessity compelled to eat. Yet they seemed to manage fairly well, and the children and workers were kept with full stomachs, though with very little variety, and no one knew what Maggie sacrificed to give to the children.

Then John was in the army, a soldier at last, and very smart his children thought him when they gazed at the tall khaki clad figure. The war years made but little impression on the children, their main memories were the nights they were allowed out to see the searchlights sweeping their silver paths in the dark sky, and the drone of the zeppelins as they soared overhead. The night when Aunty Kate came home and discovered that she had lost her railway pass that the munitions workers were given for their journey to and from the great shadow factory a few miles distant. The other children were in bed, but little Mary could not sleep until the rest of the household had retired. How well she remembered going out that night into the deserted streets, the bright moonlight making the city as bright almost as day, scanning the roadway in search of the missing scrap of pasteboard, and finding it at last on the steps of the railway station. Then the climax of the return home, to find that the cat had stolen the kippers which had been prepared for Aunty Kitty's supper as grandma had dozed off during their brief absence!

The troups of girls as they marched past in overalls and caps singing "We are the Barnbow Lassies, the Bonny Barnbow lasses!" in their way to work. The early closing of the schools in winter time. Brief visits from their father when he had leave from the army. The hectic joy of the crowds on Armistice Day, when the wounded soldiers who were staying at a temporary hospital near by, leaned out of the windows waving pillow cases, flags, and even their crutches to the deliriously happy passers by. These were the memories of the children, whom the tragedy and pain of war had left untouched, the grown ups shared in their joy, but their happiness was dulled by the pain of loss for those loved ones they would never see again.

# Chapter IV

The children grew in health and strength accepting changes as they came. The year before the war ended their grandmother had died, and the house seemed empty indeed to Maggie, as Mary had started school. She had kept her at home as long as possible, teaching the child to read and write, telling her stories from the books that Edward the elder brother had left at home when he went to seek his fortune in America. The child was nearly six when she started school, and thought it a great waste of time when she had to struggle with "pot hooks and hangers" as the teachers called the squirly figures they made on paper, when she could already form her letters. The first day at school was an embarrassing one for her. The school attendance officer who had been active in the seeking out and sending this young child to school, came along to visit the class. On finding little Mary present, he commanded her to stand on her chair, and told the other children to look at the big girl who was afraid to go to school. This injustice hurt the little girl, who had always passionately wanted to go to school, and had been kept at home by her lonely Aunt. Taunting her on being twice as big as the other children, the man enjoyed seeing the tears in the eyes of the child. If only she could have replied what she was thinking, that she was only bigger than the others because she was standing on a chair, and the others sitting down. But tongue tied and unhappy she had to stand there and hear the laughter of the other children. An unhappy episode in what should have been to her a joyful day.

The streets around were familiar to the children that Aunty Maggie cherished, and their names had a fascination for the youngest of them, Cotton Street, Wool Street, Leather Street, Flax Place, Worsted Street, all conjured in the child's mind the huge bales of stuff that came from the mills around. Then there was Foundry Street with its attendant Copper and Brass Streets. In vain did Mary search for Iron and Steel amongst the name plates at the end of the interminable rows of houses. Even the public houses, with their smell of hops and malt on brewing days, when the clouds of pungent steam rose from their cellars and filled the neighbourhood, had names connected with the city's industry, for was there not the Weavers Arms, the Silk Mill Inn, the Spinners Arms and the Woolpack. Most of the beer houses had been re-named by the local humourists and the Weavers arms was known locally as the "Shuttles" and the Spitalfield Tavern for no apparent reason was known as the "Squinting Duck".

Later in life, Mary read of the pity, kindly philanthropic people, had for the children of the slums, who played in the gutters and dirt of the pavements, and she smiled a little to herself. There was dirt in those slum streets, smells and germs also, but the children lived in a world of their own making, - those narrow ugly streets to them were mighty battle fields, the stones and dust when ground into a fine powder by another larger stone, became coloured sands of red and gold which slipped though their fingers and poured into the roadway like the sands of some far away magical desert.

The games they played in the broken down empty houses, with their crumbling walls and skeleton roofs. The boys climbing up the walls in to the rafters, loosening the wooden beams, and bringing down showers of rubble and plaster. How often had those houses been turned into strongholds and fought for by bands of excited children, until the advent of the policeman on his beat had put an end to their little war, and friend and foe alike had disappeared like chaff before the wind of the Majestic Law.

There was a beck too that ran through the streets, evil smelling and dirty, with rubbish floating on its surface. Orange boxes and rotten fruit from the markets, streams of dye which had been vomited by the mills along its banks, an occasional dead dog or cat. All these floated on its tide to join the large river which fed the town with its power, but the children were not deterred by such trifles, and spent hours piling up stepping stones to cross it when in flood, or jump from one steep slimy bank to the other often falling in and going home with wet and smelly clothes to angry parents, and perhaps a jolly good spanking, only to return next day, for all the threats of punishment in the world could not stand in the way of their pleasures of the "beck".

Despite the germs and smells the Granachan children thrived, only an occasional cold keeping them indoors for a day at the most. They did fairly well at school, Kitty perhaps being the one who learned least, as she was a veritable chatterbox and could not keep her attention on her lessons when there were more exciting things to discuss with her fellow pupils. Of course the teachers found this very exasperating and Kitty got as many canings and black marks as her sunny disposition earned her good ones.

The head mistress of the school was a nun named Sister Mary Clare, who was a very accomplished person, and she trained the children with a firm hand. When the time came for the St Patrick's Concert, she taught them to dance and sing, and picked plays for them to act in. It was wonderful the way these nuns could train the children to dance and make their costumes when they lived a life so far from worldly things. Nothing seemed impossible to them. They could paint scenery, design costumes, and contrive striking effects for the stage. It was

Sister Clare who introduced the coloured limelights that revolved on to the stage and changed the colours of the children's white dresses to the softest pinks and blues of the rainbow. The other teachers helped of course, but their home and outside interests prevented them from taking the personal interest in the children that the nuns had such a gift for.

The children's school days were punctuated by the feast days they loved, and their Aunties kept up the customs of their mother in dressing the children's hair with ribbons to suit the different Holy Days. White satin ribbons for May with its church processions, green - the true emerald for St Patrick's Day, Red for the feasts of Our Lord, and blue for the Blessed Virgin. It gave an extra joy to the holidays when the new ribbons were tied to the fair pigtails. For concerts and processions, Aunty Kitty put the children's hair in ringlets, a painful process. The long strips of cloth were put into the hair which was wound tightly round it, and then the other length was bandaged round it again, and tied firmly in place. These "sorefingers" as the children called them, were most uncomfortable, and sleep was very uneasy unless one lay on one's stomach to keep the hair away from the pillows. Kitty's hair, being soft and silky curled easily, but with Mary's coarser locks the curling was more difficult. For her the "bandages" were removed for mass on Sunday mornings, but had to be put on again before dinner or the curl would have vanished for the evening service.

There was a difference in the speech of the children of the Irish people, intonations and turns of the tongue that their Yorkshire bred companions had not. Often a friend of Mary's would try to correct her speech, as at the time when she was told "Why do you say "She does be coming down the Street"?"

"Can't you say, "She's cuming down t' street"?" That's the reight way to speak English!" Or, "Why do you Irish always say "the"?" "Close the door!  Here's the box" "Don't you know you should say Shut t' door - Heres t' box"?" - "It's only the Irish that say "the"!".  But the difference of speech made little or no alteration in their childish friendships, and they all played together when their respective schools had closed their doors upon them.

# Chapter V

One memorable year a young and zealous clergyman came to one of the neighbouring Protestant churches. Here the congregation was small, and the interest luke warm, and this enterprising young man decided to go out into the highways and byways in search of his flock. He was indefatigable and went into almost every house in the district, heedless of the religious convictions of the occupants, and exhorted them to a better way of life, inviting them to his Sunday services. Then he started open air prayer meetings, and though many came to scoff, quite a number of them stayed to listen.

He rushed around the streets wearing cassock and biretta, and through the sheer force of his personality began to fill his hitherto empty church.

On Whit Mondays it was the custom of the chief churches of the district to walk in procession with the clergy and congregation round the parishes, an occasion which was followed by a tea party and sports for the children. In the poorer districts the children all loved this Whitsuntide Holiday, for then they had on their new clothes, a thing that came to a lot of them only once a year.

In their new dresses and straw hats, the girls would go proudly to church, followed by the boys, pleasedly sheepish in their new suits, and shining creaking boots. In a parish of five thousand souls, as St Mary's had grown to be, the length of the procession was very great, and in the heat of the summer the walk became a very gruelling one, as most of the particpants were wearing new shoes. That procession was the only thing that emptied the public houses before closing time. Everyone who possibly could, lined the route to watch the procession pass, and many were the coins given to the children as they passed their grown up friends and neighbours.

Just imagine then, this great crocodile wending its way along the streets when another smaller one led by cross bearer and acolytes from the nearby protestant church, their eager clergyman urging them on, cut right through the walking children, letting the first part of the procession move on and leaving the rest waiting in consternation for the interlopers to pass.

Pandemonium broke loose! The onlookers, at that part of the route, were mostly the rougher elements of the crowd, and many of them had been drinking. They surged forward to break up the newly arrived vanguard, others tried to stop them and a free fight ensued. Fortunately, the new procession was of no great length, and had to go by almost at the double as the leaders realised the enormity of their offence. Whether it was done purposely no one ever truly found out, but it certainly caused a lot of arguments and fights for many a day to come, for in those days, very little excuse was needed to cause a riot in that neighbourhood. Later an apology was made to the clergy of St Mary's, and the zealous parson made arrangements to time his future processions so that there would be no more clashes.

There were still a lot of rough and queer characters living on the "Ham Shank", but a great many of the rogues and vagabonds had been cleared away. There were brawls on Saturday nights especially, when the men had their fill and more of beer, and fights were a weekend feature, and source of entertainment to many of the dwellers in the district. The early closing of the public houses, which had been kept open all day in the old days, put an end to a lot of drunkenness, and the place was much quieter than it had been a few years previously.

To the respectable families, living their simple lives, these brawls meant little or nothing. They kept their doors and windows shut, and soon the noise would die away as the police dispersed the crowds, and sometimes arrested the culprits. Saturdays in the Granachan household passed peacefully by. The weekend shopping was done, and the preparations for Sunday went forward. To the two little girls, Saturday night was a pleasant thing. The short walk through the darkening streets to the dimly lit church for confession. The homeward rush down the hill, to the bright kitchen fire, where there was water heating in big iron kettles for their baths. Nearby there was a house in which a white haired old lady lived, who was famous in the district for the trunnel pies she made, and for her peas, boiled in a huge pot over the fire. There the children went each Saturday night, and brought home the pies and peas for supper. After the bathing and hair washing they enjoyed the never to be forgotten taste of Mrs Welshe's pies, and went to bed in happy repletion.

After his demobilisation, John joined the great racing fraternity, and became a bookmaker. He travelled about a great deal, following the race meetings all over England, and was often away from home for a few weeks at a time. The children looked forward to his return, and there was nearly always something for them, delicious black liquorice cakes from Pontefract, packets of butterscotch from Doncaster, shortbreads from Scotland, - these things were eagerly awaited by the three children, who stood around their father as he unpacked his belongings, and with a smile and a kiss he presented their gifts to them.

The word "Bookmaker" conjures up a vision of a beefy, florid man, with a raucous voice, and an overloud taste in suits and neck ties, but John was a direct contradiction of this popular fancy. With his tall, athletic figure, his quiet well cut clothes and his pleasant voice, which never was raised above an ordinary talking pitch, his natural courtesy and air of good breeding, he soon earned for himself the soubriquet of "Gentleman John". His pleasant easy manner and also his reputation as a boxer gained him respect from the rougher elements of the racing world. His life was now completely altered, perhaps the loss of his beloved wife had made him restless, but he chose the wandering life, and it remained his mode of life for many years to come. In the same way that his mother had spoiled him the sisters carried on, although not to the extreme limits of the parental spoiling. Every whim was granted, and tiny services performed for him, so that he grew so used to being waited on hand and foot, that he took the love behind the service for granted, and expected more attention than ever.

On the children he lavished all the love of his heart spending as much time with them as his job allowed. They would sit in the evenings in the parlour, playing their simple card games, or their father would set them pages to read in turn from the few books the household possessed. In this way, the children early became aquainted with David Copperfield, Jane Eyre, and the Pickwick Papers, although it must be confessed that though the two former books made a deep impression on the children, and were never forgotten friends of Mary at least, the illustrations of the latter had far more effect on the children, than the words of the author which were rather a little way above their heads.

Then there were the lovely surprise days, when John would pack the children into one of the new charabancs, and would take them to see the beauty spots of Yorkshire. The beauty of the wooded hills of Knaresborough with its broad river, its magical wishing well, with the petrified articles hanging in the caves. Old Mother Shipton's cave, which gave the children a delicious fearful thrill, as they peered around, half expecting to see the old woman creep out of some dark and secret corner. Then tea in the House on the Hill, built into the rocky side of the mountain. The broad streets of lordly Harrogate, with its great hotels and magnificent lawns. The crooked little streets of York, where they walked along the Roman Walls, or gazed in awe at the majestic Minster, lost in the silence of its great aisles and the solemn grandeur of its almost heavenly height. Climbing the steep streets of Ilkley to roam the towering moors dancing on the springy turf, or squelching through its hidden streamlets. Those were the days when the children loved to be with their father, and all was right with the world.

But those days could not be repeated often, as school and work came first, so the children spent more time with their young companions and their Aunts than they did with John, their father. Kate as always, was the favourite playtime Aunt. On the long winter evenings, around the fire, with the curtains drawn, they would sit, roasting potatoes or chestnuts at the glowing grate, listening to Aunty Kitty telling her tales or reciting the poems she had learned at school. Oh! the solemn almost tearful faces of the children as she declaimed in deep sepulchral tones, "The Inchcape Bell", or the screams of laughter that followed the one about the "old man who wouldn't say his prayers" - putting the words of the song by seizing the nearest leg, to "Throw him down the stairs". Never was little Mary in later years to take the poker

in hand to stir the blaze, without that ghost of a beloved voice whispering in her ear "Poke, poke the fire up".

*Make a pretty light,*
*Here comes a little girl, dressed all in white,*
*White shoes and stockings on, white curly hair,*
*A little muffler round her neck, and her Sunday*
*hat she'll wear".*

That was one of their favourite rhymes, and always sung when the fire was stirred by the shining black poker with the gleaming brass handle.

It was a pleasure also to go out for walks with Aunty Kate, there was never anything too much trouble for her. Walks to the parks or trams into the country side, with always a certainty of a bag of sweets or ice creams on the way. She always went to mass on Sundays to the church at which she had attended in her younger days - St Patrick's and often would take one of the children with her. Then on the way home they would call at the ice cream shop for a "pie" dyed crimson with splashes of sarsparilla, or yellow with lemon flavouring. Kindly Aunt Kate,was the childrens companion in fun, for she had never quite grown up herself.

Of the Aunts, Mary was perhaps the least intimate with the children, for she was very possessive in her love, and the healthy young animal in the children shrank from too many demonstrations of love, but she bought them - the most expensive of their toys, and always gave generously to them when extra expenses were incurred. By this time she had become deeply religious, and almost everything she said and did was bound up with the Catholic

Faith. If the children wanted to know anything about the lives of the saints, they went to her for information, as the drawers in her room were full of books and pamphlets or Holy pictures.

# Chapter VI

The passing of the years had brought changes to the family, and the three sisters who had been so carefree in their youth; perhaps it should be said, the two eldest had been carefree, for responsibilities and care had fallen more heavily on Maggie, though she had been the "baby" of the family, were now staid and plain women who spent nearly all their spare time at home. Perhaps the difference in appearance was more noticeable in the once so slim Kate. Whilst working in a shell factory during the war, a shell case had fallen on her foot, crushing the big toe, and after weary months, when she was unable to walk, she put on weight and was now utterly changed from the thin light of foot creature she had been. The injury to her foot was to affect her for the rest of her life, and for several years, she walked slowly and with difficulty, her increased weight adding to her burden. Her dress was plain, and without the fashionable flair of other days.

Mary too had altered, gone was the proud beauty of her youth, although she had never lost the erect and graceful carriage which had earned the name of "Princess" from the children in bygone days. Maggie too was buxom, the brown curls gone, her hair almost black, parted in the middle and worn, smoothly brushed away from the wide forehead. With the years her face had taken on a patient sweetness, a saintly quality which all the friends of the children, and others who saw her, compared to pictures of the Madonna.

Spinsters they were, plain in their dress and homely in their ways, but never would they become that type designated as "old maids". Children were always welcomed at their home, nothing they could do or any of their naughtiness tried the patience of the sisters. Once Maggie was heard to say on seeing a child weep

"Never do anything to take the smile from a child's face" and indeed she seemed to model her life on those words. If patience is a virtue then surely the patience of Aunty Maggie would get her a front seat in Heaven.

The children too, were growing up, Edward had left school and was working in a butcher's shop. His various escapades did not keep him long there. The first wage he drew, he spent on the way home, buying himself a huge cheap pocket watch and chain, which was promptly confiscated by Aunty Mary, and taken back to the shop. The manager for whom he worked was a kindly man, and took the boy under his wing, but his sudden death made changes necessary and soon Edward was out of a job.

He got another position, as errand boy at a pork shop, but lost that job under rather amusing circumstances. He was wheeling a cart load of pork pies through one of the Jewish quarters of the town and could not resist jeering at the Jewish boys, asking them if they were jealous of him having all those pork pies, which they could not eat. After some altercation the Jews retaliated; they overturned the cart, and all the delicious pies went rolling in the gutters. It's needless to say, Edward did not return for his job!

Kitty too was growing up, although her stature was still tiny. She looked thin and delicate, although her cheeks were round and rosy, but she was wiry and a veritable tomboy. Not for Kitty were the more ladylike shuttle cocks and battledores of her sister Mary, - Kitty liked to play with the lads at "taws", and her knees and knuckles bore witness to the fact. As Sister Paul, one of her teachers remarked to Aunty Maggie, "If Kitty talked less, and kept still for a while, maybe she'd grow fatter, but she wore her jaws out with chattering and the flesh off her bones with her incessant running about". But of the three children, Kitty did the most worrying about other people. When her father was away she continually wondered where he was and how he was faring. Always the first to greet him when he came home, and ask him if he had done well or ill. Always the one to take his morning tea and newspaper to him after his late journeys, her father was the centre of her life. The more phlegmatic Mary took his absences for granted, and as she prayed for his safety left the rest to God. Whether he had made money or lost it never entered her head, as money had no interest for her, and indeed she was to display this trait almost all her life. Her affections were slower than Kitty's more mercurial passions, and her hatreds and dislikes were non existent. Kitty either loved or detested, Mary just liked or was supremely indifferent. As sisters they were the antithesis of each other.

In the earlier years of childhood, Mary had clung to Edward more than to her sister. What ever he did was right to her, and she believed that he could do anything on earth. He looked after his baby sister, and made desks and blackboards for her, as her one passion was to be a teacher. When Edward decided that he could make a piano out of an old dresser and some wires, Mary firmly believed that he could do it, and could not understand Aunty Maggie's laughter, or her refusal to give them the dresser for Edward's experiment. On one occasion, the children were left alone in the house, (for the first and last time) as Maggie had gone to the neighbouring shops. They found a short length of rubber hose, and Edward began to demonstrate the change of steam into water. Putting one end of the hose to the spout of the boiling kettle, he told Kitty to put her face to the other end and feel the cold water coming out of the pipe. Unfortunately the experiment didn't turn out as anticipated, and Maggie rushed into the house on hearing Kitty's screams, to find her cheek scalded with the hot steam and water. It was a painful experiment for Kitty, but Mary knew in her heart that the water must have been at fault, for did not Edward say it should be cold water, and what Edward said, was right!

It was heavenly for her to go to mass with Edward, where they would usually sit behind a pillar, and eat the sweets he had bought on the way. How often in the middle of the sermon had he to nudge her for her enthusiastic sucking of her toffee, as the frowns of their neighbours spoke their disapproval.

So the children grew, each in their different ways, Edward with his love for woodwork and his ear for music, his bursts of enthusiasm for jobs that never made a success. Kitty with her chattering tongue and worrying heart, Mary with her love of books that never was and perhaps never would be satisfied and her placid nonchalant affections, under the care of their three aunts and the erratic surveillance of their father.

The district did not change a great deal, though it was quieter and much more respectable than when the child Maggie had come to live there. The older fighting stock had died out, but still there were occasional brawls, but to these the family turned a deaf ear and a blind eye. The interests of the women folk centred mostly round the church, and schools, these being the central points of their lives, and the aunts relived the days of their youth, as they watched young Kitty and Mary set out for the school treats and church festivals. The high light of the year was the procession which celebrated the feast of Corpus Christi. Then the church grounds were gaily decorated with flags and bunting, and an altar erected on the lawn behind the presbytery. Nearly all the congregation walked in outdoor procession and people came from far and near to see it. The school girls in their white dresses, the boys in their white shirts and red sashes, the children of Mary in their blue cloaks and white veils, the young men and old, the mothers of the parish, and then the Guard of Honour with their drawn swords walking beside the silken canopy, before which picked girls from the orphanage strewed flower petals, and under the canopy the priest carrying the Blessed Sacrament, to the altar in the grounds for benediction in the open air. Then the sweet notes of the O Salutaris would rise on the evening air, and the responses sound from a thousand throats dying away to silence only broken by the rustling trees and the carrolling birds as they gave accompaniment to the silver booming of the sanctuary gong.

It has been said that only in the poorer districts was such ritual liked, and that the poorer the neighbourhood the higher the church ritual, be that true or not, the colour and pageantry of that Corpus Christi procession put a new beauty into the lives of the people of drab slums and uplifted them with an almost unearthly devotion.

There were the jolly Guild Meetings too, where games were played and the children met their friends away from the dangers of the streets. "Duck apple night" the feast of all hallowe'en, was a night looked forward to by Kitty and Mary. There in the schoolroom were bowls of water, with rosy apples reposing at the bottom. There the spluttering children tried to grasp the apples in their teeth, swallowing mouthfuls of water in the attempt. Or the apples were suspended on pieces of string, and amidst bursts of laughter the girls with their hands clasped behind their backs would pursue the elusive fruit with craning necks and snapping teeth. The unsuccessful ones were given their apples from the large baskets, so none of them went home dissatisfied with the evening's fun.

*East Street · Photographic Collection Leeds Public Library & Local History Department*

*Steander, Timble Beck · Photographic Collection Leeds Public Library & Local History Department*

*Tab Street · Photographic Collection Leeds Public Library & Local History Department*

*Corpus Christie Procession Mount St. Mary's c. 1928 · Photograph unknown*

*Rooke's Fold, The Bank 1903· Photographic Collection Leeds Public Library & Local History Department*

*Silk Mill Inn, Mill Street · Photographic Collection Leeds Public Library & Local History Department*

# The Ham Shank

*Well Houses · Photographic Collection Leeds Public Library & Local History Department*

# Chapter VII

During the great national slump period, unemployment was rife in the district, and the street corners were propped up daily by the men who had no work. The daily trek to the Labour Exchange by groups of shabby men, was a usual sight, and the children watched these men change from cheerful workers into apathetic creatures who hung about the streets, reading the "Tisher" as they called the "Sporting Pink" racing papers, in an endeavour to find winners to supplement their meagre supply of money. That they did sometimes back winners was testified by the queues that stood outside the street bookmaker's house at paying out time.

Another way of swelling their incomes were the "tossing schools", usually held in the middle of the street, where the men gathered in a circle, with a man on look out for the police, and by tossing pennies for heads and tails tried their chances with lady luck. The children playing near by, heard the jargon of these men, but it meant little to them "heads a tanner!" "tails a deemer" "heads a bob" were called out by the men, and sometimes higher stakes were used. Indeed some men who made a business of these gambling schools often returned home richer by several pounds.

On the advent of the police the men would take to their heels, and as often happened in a surprise visit from the law, the money stakes which had been placed on the roadway were scattered by the running men, and the children would scramble for the rolling coins. Often the men would run into neighbouring houses and would be sitting at the table joining in the family meals or coatless sitting near the fire, deep in the newspaper when the suspicious policemen came inquiring after the runaways. When some unfortunate gambler was caught, and the police frogmarched him to the local police station, they would be followed by jeering crowds who by jostling the representatives of the law, and even stoning them, often succeeded in helping the captive to escape. Often on snowy Sunday mornings as Kitty and Mary were going to church they saw these men cleaning a circle in the roadway in preparation for their day's gambling. Rough in their speech and scoffers at religion as most of these men were, they always had a respect for the church goers, and often would modify their profane language when the children passed to go to mass, with a smile and a touch of their shabby caps as they heard the cheerful "Good Morning" of the youthful voices.

There was a young man who spent his whole free time in the service of Mount St Marys. He trained the altar boys and was master of ceremonies at all the services. His extreme piety was lightened by a sense of humour, and often he surprised strangers by his broad views, which were unexpected in one of such deep religious convictions. The gamblers knew him and perhaps his manner of life annoyed them, so they started to call him "the little priest", and they were not alone in this as it was a favourite name for the young man amongst many who knew him. One Sunday morning as he passed them they all solemnly doffed their caps and with exaggerated politeness said to him "Good Morning Father". George's face lit up with an impish smile "Good Morning, children" said he, and strode blithely on. The gamblers never pulled his leg again

When Mary was nearly twelve years old, she started going to the college attached to the church. Earlier Kitty had had the chance to go, but at the last minute shyness swamped her and she elected to stay on at the elementary school. To Mary, it was the beginning of a new life. Always a lover of literature, she could now steep herself in the great writers and poets as never before, and for a child of her age, had read and loved her books, with an interest unusual in one so young. It did not take her long to settle down at her new school and the teacher who was foremost in her affections was the literature mistress, Sister Mary Angela, this being the natural consequence of their mutual love of books, and the nun encouraged Mary in her studies of the poets.

The headmistress at the time was a palefaced dignified nun, named Sister Marcella, and all the girls admired her, although they stood in awe of her cold and dignified manner. When she took the history classes however, the awe faded, and only the pictures of the past which she so vividly painted were seen by the interested girls.

It was not a large building in comparison with some of the secondary schools of the city, but it was cleanly and beautifully built, with shining parquet floors, and glass partitioned rooms. There were boarding pupils too, from all parts of England, and the British Isles, the majority of them hailing from Ireland. Some few, came from further abroad, indeed one of the girls came from South America. The day pupils were segregated from the boarders as much as possible which was resented by the day pupils, who only in after years could see the wisdom of this, and often there were quarrels between the two factions when the teacher in charge was absent for a time. Perhaps the best loved teacher at the College was the French and Art mistress, a German nun named Sister Carmel. She was a very accomplished person, a good artist, pianist and the possessor of a glorious singing voice. All the girls, with perhaps the exception of Mary chose her as their favourite, but her strident laughter, which rose at the slightest provocation, and her complete enjoyment of her own jokes, annoyed the girl and perhaps were the foundation for her not quite taking this teacher to her heart as the other pupils declared they had.

Sister Bernardine, clever and shy, who swept into rooms like a tornado, and could read in Latin Grammars backwards, and upside down, always able to point out from any angle the place at which some floundering pupil had stopped in state of tonguetied anxiety or giggling futility, according to her temperament. Sister Mary of the Nativity, grey eyed and humourous, who took the Science classes, shrewdly choosing the most mischevious of her pupils to carry out special experiments, knowing full well it was the best way to keep them quiet. Sister Bernard, strict and sarcastic who took mathematics with almost military precision. Sister Gerard, who took the music classes, and with the aid of a beautiful gramophone and even lovelier records awakened in even the most unmusical of her pupils the love of good music, and gave them a nodding acquaintance with the old masters. Gentle Sister Lucilla, the teacher of domestic science, whom the wilder of the pupils flouted unmercifully, until she turned from a lamb into a veritable lioness. These, and others were the teachers at the college, and under their tuition the girls grew in knowledge and good health.

From a shy retiring child Mary changed with the years and became the ringleader of most of the mischief in her class, and there were times when she must have tried the patience of her teachers sorely. The day she put her head inside the fume cupboard when they were preparing chlorine, and one of the other girls pulled the shutter down, guillotine-wise over the back of her neck, and she was sent out, spluttering and coughing on to the fire escape to get some fresh air, gave no annoyance to Sister Nativity, but only deepened the twinkle in those dark grey eyes. Once, the girls procured some white face powder and carefully rubbed it into Mary's rosy cheeks, and she was excused classes and sent to rest, her friends periodically and solicitiously coming to visit her, collapsing in laughter on arrival at the sight of her sickly face. Happy, innocent days, of fun and learning, of tramping to the sports field, or kneeling before the altar in the Convent Chapel to hear the Bishop, who always came to visit them on their speech day, which was their special day, the Feast of the Immaculate Conception. Dear children's Bishop, Dr Cowgill, who knew almost every child by his own favourite name, always calling Mary his little "Rosy Cheeks".

On that special day the girls gave a concert and their parents or any old pupils were allowed to attend. The musical section formed an orchestra, and the good singers a choir. After the concert and speeches, the Bishop usually sang the song demanded of him, year after year, and there he would stand, his eyes dancing beneath his snow white brows, singing in a tuneless voice "The funniest feller that ever I saw, was the feller that looked like me".

Reverend Mother, with her rosy cheeks and skin like a young girl's, with her white curls which willfully strayed beneath the white linen of her coif, sat happy and beaming, amongst the other nuns, in the audience for this special occasion.

How different from this peaceful simple atmosphere was life outside the walls which secluded the Convent, Church and Schools. The busy streets teeming with life, their noise and smells contrasting oddly with the cleanliness and quiet of the hill, as the children came out of school and church to clatter down the cobbled ways, their shrill voices filling the air and drowning the duller tones of the mills and factories. The cool air on the hill top lost itself amongst the stifled houses, and in summer the people sat out on their doorsteps, or brought their chairs on to the pavement to escape the close atmosphere of their tiny homes, the children playing in the streets long after bedtime, because they would not be able to sleep in their overcrowded bedrooms.

Some of the luckier ones had spent their annual holidays at the sea side, but the greater number did not go far from home, except for a day at the city parks or on a trip to the sea. One of the features of the district was the excursions run by the public houses, and the customers, after paying their subscriptions, were in high spirits. The "charas" came to a standstill outside the "pub" in question, and then the fun began.

Crates of bottled beer would be handed into the coach, and then the trippers, all in their "Sunday best", with added trimmings by way of rosettes and fancy hats would follow accompanied by the cheers and ribald jests of the friends they were leaving behind. Showers of coppers would be flung out for the children, and a mad scramble would ensue. Then with a blowing of horns the revellers would move off. The return journey was eagerly awaited, and the patrons who had stayed behind, loitered after "closing time" for the return of the "chara". The hoots and laughter the slurred speech and lurching gait of the trippers, together with the alcoholic smell as they tumbled from the coach spoke volumes of the "good time" they had had. Often an argument had started on the way home, and then the antagonists would face each other to finish the row, sometimes relenting to the pleas of their wives or friends not "to spoil a good day", or, more often infuriated by interference would start a free for all fight, as a fitting finish to a "perfect day!"

The Granachan family did not go away for holidays, despite the pleading of the children, for their father was always too busy with his racing journeys to take them, and the aunts were too shy to stay anywhere than in their own house, so day trips to Scarborough or Blackpool were the limit of their journeyings. The sight of the sea, seen unexpectedly as young Mary glanced between two old shops in Scarborough gave her a decided thrill. Just for a moment the patch of sea with its one visible sailing boat and the cloudy sky hung motionless as a seascape, framed in the walls of the two houses. Mary stopped and stared, thinking that she was looking at some large painting, breathless with the beauty of it. "Look! there's the sea!" an excited voice cried, and the spell was broken. The white sail stirred in the breeze and the waves continued their perpetual motion, it was the sea indeed - the real live sea, but it did not hold the same thrill for her as in that split second she had caught its arrested motion in an enchanted moment of perfect beauty.

# Chapter VIII

John, by this time was an eternally busy man, always he had appointments with his friends and acquaintances of the racing world, and was continually rushing into the house in a tearing hurry, and rushing out again. There was never a time that he wasn't an hour late to catch a train or half an hour late for one of his various dates, or, so he would state as he demanded attention from the household.

"Mary, brush your father's hat, Kitty, here are his handkerchiefs, Edward, remind your dad to pack his hairbrushes, John have you got your shaving things?" At these moments, Aunty Maggie was in a ferment, trying to remember little details that she knew John would forget. The children, mobilised to cope with the rush, ran upstairs and down, noting each item, whilst John packed his bags in a frenzy, glancing every two minutes at his watch to satisfy himself that he was really late. Then with everything complete, he would hug and kiss the girls, and give a parting pat to Edward, if he was present, and grasping his suitcase would go at top speed from the house. Always in a hurry, stirring the calm waters of the household to a racing torrent, yet he never missed a train in his life, despite his protestations that he "should have been at the station an hour ago!" - leaving the others at home limp and exhausted, but glad of the peace that descended when he at last rushed from the house. Often men would come to see him when he was spending any short stay at home, his clerks and "tick tacks" or men who did odd jobs for him - for John loved to be waited on, and always found someone willing to carry his racing equipment or run errands for him. He issued orders like some field marshal, and the others listened with great respect. When the children grew up, they saw the humour of many a situation in which their father marshalled his men, almost making them stand to attention, and their merry eyes would challenge the grave faces of the men who listened so earnestly to their father's repeated orders. All these men had a great liking for John, and so they let him order them about knowing that his manner hid a heart that was as soft as his manner was peremptory.

Sometimes he was accompanied home by his friends after a convivial evening, and if the children were in sight, their hands would be filled with shillings and even half crowns that the men thrust upon them, despite their polite refusals. On one occasion, one of the men, whom they had known from babyhood and called Uncle Charlie emptied the entire contents of his pockets on to the table, and insisted that the children should share the money. The amount came to over six pounds, so Aunty Maggie confiscated it, and returned it to the man the next day. He sent the children five shillings each, to make up for their loss of the whole amount, which he was glad enough to have back again when he was sober!

They were real rough diamonds, these men of the racing world, hard drinking, gambling men, with rough tongues and happy go lucky ways, but their generosity hid a multitude of their faults. If one of them was ill or otherwise unable to earn his living, they would all get together and start a fund which helped to tide the unfortunate man's wife and family over the difficult period. Their money came and vanished in an almost miraculous way. Sometimes John would arrive home after a good day with his pocket full of money, and after giving up an adequate sum for household expenses would perhaps give Maggie a large amount of money to put away for him. It was a large amount to a working class family, sometimes reaching three figures. By the end of the week it had all gone, - lost at the next race meeting that came along.

Sometimes he would come home, cold and wet to the skin, as the weather had been bad, and they had stood all day shivering in the cold winds and pouring rain. Yet these men were hardy, their open air life giving them an impervious resistance to the inclemencies of the English climate, and after a good hot meal and change of clothing they were none the worse for their ordeal.

They were mostly honest men, but there were the rogues of their little world, the "racing tykes" as they called the card sharpers, pick pockets and hoodlums of the race tracks. Yet, even amongst these men there was a certain code of honour, and men they knew and respected were left unmolested by them. On one occasion an acquaintance of John, was with him on one of the racecourses, ostentatiously displaying a large gold chain to which was attached an equally expensive gold watch. In vain did John advise him to keep close to him and avoid the crowds at the turnstiles, as he may find that his watch and chain were missing when he reached his destination. Self assured and just a trifle scornful, the friend replied that he could take care of himself, and confidently mixed with the crowd. When they met at the railway platform the other man stood raging and upset, minus his precious watch and chain. After extracting a promise from the subdued man, that he would be careful in future and would take no proceedings against the pickpocket if John found him, they got on to their train and were soon homeward bound. On reaching the home station, John stopped a little fellow who was also pursuing his homeward way. After a few words the little man handed to John's friend his lost property saying "I'm sorry John, I didn't know he was a pal of yours, but he shouldn't have b— well shown off so much with his b— watch and chain!" There was nothing these men respected as genuine honesty, such as John's - but heaven help the "suckers" when they were abroad!

The tale was told of one of the men who refused to pay a bet to a punter, and after an altercation he said "Oh go away - before I spit in your eye!" "If you spit as straight as you bet", replied the irate backer, " then go ahead and spit!" He was paid out by the discomfited bookie.

Edward was trying hard to follow in his father's footsteps, much to the consternation of his aunts, who disapproved of such a mode of life. He got a job, taking bets from street bookies to the central offices, rushing round the neighbourhood at tremendous speed on a bicycle, to get the bets in before the race times. He was no respecter of persons or things, and pedestrians had to scatter before him. On several occasions he angered the housewives by cycling through their lines of washing when the clothes lines were lowered for the taking in of the wash. One day an irate woman awaited him, and as he rode towards the lowered washing she jerked the pulley, and the line caught him by the throat, throwing him off the bicycle. He had a nasty bruise on his throat for days afterwards, but it is doubtful if it stopped his mad careering!

Then, the bicycle not taking him fast enough, he bought a motor cycle, and the noise of his engine as he rushed past the house almost every half hour, made poor Aunty Maggie's heart rush into her mouth several times in a day.

The children indeed were altering and growing up fast, but the aunts did not change. The two eldest still worked in the woollen mills, wearing their big black shawls over their heads, and the harding aprons of their former days, the baskets in which they took their food hanging from their arms. Mary seldom went out, unless it was to church in the evenings, and Maggie could not be persuaded to go anywhere for an hour's pleasure. Always she had the excuse of work to do in the home. It was remarkable, that, although she seldom went away from the house, she was conversant with current affairs, and had an intelligent grasp on the politics of the country. Her general knowledge too was remarkable, and the children, on finding difficulties with their lessons, always found the correct answers were given by Aunty Maggie. If life had called her to a different sphere she would have been a brilliant woman, but her innate shyness and the force of circumstances compelled her to "hide her light under a bushel". So life passed her by, or did she turn her back upon it? Was she aware of the tremendous sacrifice she had made, spending the years in cooking and scrubbing and washing for the family that had come to depend on her? Or in her humility did she accept all this as her proper station in life? The answer to those questions lie, deep and unanswered in her patient heart.

Kate was still the liveliest of the sisters, and often took the children for jaunts in the country, or on visits to the picture palaces which had sprung up in the district. There they would sit in the dark, watching the ghostly figures flit jerkily across the screen, in those pioneer days of the silent films, laughing and weeping with Charlie Chaplin, sighing with Nazimova, cheering enthusiastically with the rest of the audience when at last the hero came to the rescue of the much ill used heroine, jeering at the violent end of the villain of the piece.

Often the children would enact these scenes in the streets, they and their playmates taking the different parts. On one never to be forgotten occasion young Mary, as Pearl White, the film star, was tied to a lamp post and left there by the villains of the game. Unfortunately some other game caught the fancy of the other children, and they went off elsewhere to play, completely forgetting the plight of their former "heroine". After what seemed hours to the tied up child, one of the women in the street noticed her, and came to the rescue, cutting the rope from round the aching arms, and giving her a slice of jam and bread to stop the flowing tears.

The shops around had their places in the hearts of the children, each one having its speciality to tempt the pennies from their not too reluctant palms. There was liquorice and dusty locusts to be bought at Murphy's. Toffee apples and huge jaffa oranges, from which the demic parts had been cut at "Toffee Clara's". Sticky toffee filled with peanuts at Cook's, monkey nuts by the bagful at Motley's, and several other sticky varieties that tickle a childs palate at the other shops. Friday night, when the weekend pennies were given to the children were spent in a pilgrimage from shop to shop, as the children gazed at their favourite sweetmeats, in a pleasureable agony of anticipation, and indecision, the coppers growing warm and moist in their tightly clenched hands. There could be a dish of good fruit lying waiting at home, but Mary preferred the "specked oranges" from "Toffee Clara's", they were juicy and sweet, yet gave out a bitter taste that no other oranges could ever have. Most of the shops she associated with amusing remarks, made in all seriousness, as, when she went into one to buy some cakes for tea, and was told that the "three cornered squares were very nice" or when enquiring at another if they had any of those chocolates at sixpence a quarter?, was told no, they only had those at three ha'pence an ounce.

There were times when the mischievous children tried to pull the legs of the shopkeepers, dashing in to ask if they had any

"Wild Woodbines" and on getting an affirmative reply, would cry "Well, tame 'em then" and would run out again hooting with laughter. On enquiring politely at the fish and chip shops if they had "any tails please" would tell the man behind the counter to "wag 'em". The shopkeepers were used to these episodes and either laughed or exploded in wrath according to their temperaments.

The children of the district were a mixed lot, some well fed and clad, others ill nourished and neglected, but they all found a common brotherhood as they played in the streets, and sat side by side in the schools. For most of the parents of the better kept children, life was one long struggle against dirt and vermin, for the neglected children passed their heritage on to the others. The worst hours that young Kitty and Mary spent were when their long hair was thoroughly inspected by lynx eyed Aunt Kate, and vermin destroying pomade was rubbed into their scalps as a preventative of anything worse to come. Their golden hair, long and thick was the pride and joy of Aunt Kate, and she looked after it jealously, always declaring in later years, when cutting had altered the style, and its golden sheen had darkened, that it never had been the same since she had stopped looking after it, when the girls were old enough to dress their own hair themselves.

# ChapterIX

Time came along for Kitty to leave school, but John refused to believe that this, the smallest of his children, was ready to go out into the world to earn her own living, so she returned to school for another term, or so, when all her classmates had started work in the factories. Indeed, with her small stature and long plaits, she looked too young and frail to be ready to face the world, but in due course had to leave the school, and found a job in a clothing factory, nominally as a booker, but spending most of her time running errands and "mashing" teas for the older workers. When the child, for she was no more, of fourteen went into the factory she was fascinated with the very sight of it. The long building, windowless almost, the light penetrating through the glass skylights which ran the length of the roof, with its rows of sewing machines whirring under the deft manipulation of the machinists. The heaps of clothing in various stages of manufacture. The tailors sitting crosslegged on their tables, sewing with unimaginable speed. The Hoffman presses with their clouds of steam and perspiring operators, the heavy pressing irons, with their gas jets heating them, swung with ease and dexterity by their skilled users, the groups of girls and women stitching the armholes, or sewing on buttons as though their lives depended on their speed, as indeed their means of livelihood did, and above all, the close, oppressive atmosphere, redolent of grease, the limey tang of the linings, the woolly smell of the cloth and the overpowering odour of hard working humanity. Soon however she felt at home in these strange surroundings, the people in the factory always having time to spare for a word and joke with little Kitty. Many were the tears she shed at first, when she was berated for mistakes she made, or some bad tempered person vented their spleen on her defenceless head, but in a few weeks she had summoned up her courage - which she had in no small amount, and by means of cheeky answers and flashes of her

own temper, made her life easier, and won the respect of her fellow workers, who demanded that even the smallest of them must stand up for their rights, and show some spark of independence, however slight.

Mary was still at the College, doing well on all subjects but mathematics, which perhaps was the most important of all. Easy going and full of fun, she went through life there with a laugh, and indeed wasted time she should have spent in garnering knowledge, in playing pranks with those schoolfellows who were of the same temperament as herself.

Although great improvements had been made in the centre of the city, they did not affect the "Ham Shank". In fact the contrast of the widening of the main streets of the city, and the demolition of those cramped and tumbledown shops which had so delighted the heart of the "little Maggie" of those years so long ago, emphasised the narrowness of the streets and the crumbling alleyways, the shabby houses and squalid courts. The Bank had not grown in beauty with the passing years, and bore no sign of dignity which age brings to the happy and contented. Instead it had the dusty leering look of an old drunken roué who, staggering along in his cups, had collected on his garments the dust of the road, and shabbied his appearance by his own general behaviour. The streets seemed to shrink within themselves, knowing their shabby appearance, which even new coats of paint could not hide, for the crumbling brickwork and worn stone, testified to a life of hard labour, finished, and ready for a long deep rest.

The people went about their work, noticing little of the appearance of the neighbourhood, as children see only their mother's face, and notice not the lines of care etched upon it, and indeed there was little they could do to improve things. Most of the windows were neatly curtained and the steps scrubbed and sandstoned, the houses as a whole kept clean and tidy, but there were sluttish housewives in the neighbourhood who could spoil the appearance of their neighbour's houses, by their neglect of their own.

The Granachan family were well known and respected in the neighbourhood, perhaps with the exception of Edward, who although fairly popular was regarded as something of a harum scarum as he careered the streets on his motor cycle. Many people came to Aunty Maggie with their troubles and difficulties. She always listened with a sympathetic ear to tales of woe which were poured out to her, and often the troubled ones went away comforted, and with help in a practical form jingling in their pockets.

Wives, whose husbands had come home drunk and had tried to smash their houses up, and now in jail because the police had taken them away, came to borrow the money to "bail their husbands out", and despite the growing Mary's assertions that they should be left in jail, Maggie would think only of the children living without their father's money to help them, and would give the troubled wife the necessary amount. It was useless to point out to her that the husband would do the same thing again as soon as he could get hold of enough money to get drunk again. "Maybe so", she would say "But if we can help any one at all, even if we can't see any results, we might have done some little good for them!"

There were the gypsy pedlars and the old men selling bootlaces and buttons, all came and never were refused, often enjoying a cup of tea to help them on their way. The women who sold vegetables and borrowed the money weekly to buy their stock, returning it out of their earnings, only to borrow it again the following week. Then there were the children who came to visit Aunty Maggie. With pale faces and running noses, rosy cheeks and the same type of nose, tear stained or grumbling, well dressed or ragged, they all received a warm welcome, and would sit on the kitchen window sill munching reflectively the piece of cake or the sweets she would give them, watching her go about her work with the all seeing eyes of childhood.

The tiny square of uncultivated garden also attracted these children, who saw so little of the grassy fields and tall trees of the country, this grassy plot, with its couple of elder trees and thousands of huge weeds which grew as tall and even taller than the surrounding wall, was a veritable park indeed. Two tiny tots, brother and sister, who had just come to live in the district came to visit the park daily, sitting solemnly on the grass, or trotting up the path to sit on the front steps. Although they were pretty children, and very fat, they were the possessors of legs that were bowed to the extreme, and they rocked about from side to side as they walked, the miracle of them keeping their balance at all, striking any observer.

Imagine Aunty Maggie's consternation one day, when, as these two children were paying her their customary visit, the garden gate was thrust open by a representative of the N.S.P.C.C. who demanded to know why she had let her children's legs get into such a condition, and insisted that she should have them seen to immediately! Putting the official firmly in her place, Aunty Maggie refused to help her in finding the address of the children, and the discomfited woman withdrew taking a child by each hand, to start a search for the erring parents, looking like some majestic ship in full sail, accompanied by a couple of rolling porpoises. Whether the Society did take the children in hand we shall never know, but they are grown up and their legs today are perfectly straight.

Another child named Georgie, with a merry face, who was the imp of the neighbourhood also took a violent fancy to her, and he would sit for hours watching her work, prattling away to her. As his mother remarked, the only time she was easy in her mind about Georgie was when he was sitting there, as he would be up to some mischief otherwise. His mother was ill, and one day said to him "Georgie, what would you do if I should die?" "Go and live at Granachans" came the prompt reply. The unfortunate woman did not live long after that, but little Georgie did not realise his ambition as his father removed from the neighbourhood soon after, taking his family with him. But Georgie still remembered, and as soon as he was old enough to find his way back, he started visiting Aunty Maggie again.

# Chapter X

Life went on, showing its bright and its seamy side. In a district of such mixed people, there were several characters who stood out alone, and a few of these were well known to the children, who followed them about jeering, or just watched them in fascinated silence. There were low women, living in the common lodging houses, who had fallen into the depth of degradation; they frequented a small park nearby, and the curious children went along sometimes to look fearfully at them, as they sat on the wooden benches, their mottled faces and red rimmed eyes (sewn up with red cotton - was the local description) their shabby clothes and furtive scratchings at their necks and backs, and in their unkempt tousled hair, occasionally taking a drink from bottles of methylated spirits, as they were barred from the public houses, and could not get alcohol any other way. To the watching children, these creatures were hardly human, and, if one of them stirred from her lethargy to call epithets after them, they would run away as though a thousand devils were after them.

"Loppy Alice" as one of these women was known, spoke with a cultured accent, which betrayed a decent birth, but with her tawdry clothes and broken shoes, and continually searching hands for the fleas she carried on her person, was a sight which even the children felt was pitiful though disgusting. One of her friends was a pale faced tiny creature, somewhat cleaner in her dress and habits, who was known as "Piano Annie". The legend went that at some time she had been a brilliant pianist, until an accident had robbed her of several fingers, and now she knocked out tunes in any public house that would admit her, for the price of a night's free drink. Gone are those pitiful creatures, at rest now from the gibes and stares of the passersby. No one will ever know the story of their tragedies, but we must all, with Bobbie Burns bow our heads and say,

*"So at the balance, lets be mute,*
*We never can ajist it*
*Whats done, we partly may compute,*
*But know not, whats resisted"*

There were humorous characters too, who lived their lives to suit themselves, and cared for no one else's opinion. The groups of women who spent all their days drinking, from the pubs opening to closing, and during the closed period would congregate in the houses of some of them to continue their feast, the repititious journeyings of one of them to and from the back door of the nearest public house, with a large jug under her apron, taking a furtive sip before she got in sight of her comrades. Where they got the money for so much beer, or could afford this continuous round of drinking none of their more abstemious neighbours could imagine, but the weekly visits to the pawn shop gave one answer.

The gift of happy living in such a quarter was the ability to mind one's own business, a quality much respected, and one that the Granachan family possessed; even though Aunty Maggie was the recipient of so many confidences, she never was known to repeat gossip, or condemn anyone for their faults. Always she could find a sympathetic word or excuse for the frailties of those she knew, often putting in a chastening word to the outspoken criticisms of the younger members of the family, who saw the ills around them with the merciless clarity of youth. For a person of her secluded life, she was seldom shocked when the broader issues of sex were spoken about, and could always keep command of the situation, even in the most embarrassing circumstances.

One day, a woman came to the kitchen window, hawking her fruit and vegetables. She had come for years, and always, even with a well stocked larder Maggie made some small purchase from her. The woman in question was a handsome buxom creature, with a wealth of golden brown wavy hair, and bright blue eyes, her ruddy complexion showing the glowing health she enjoyed. Her husband owned a horse and cart, and hawked his wares in other districts of the city. This particular day her smile was broader than ever, her face alight with joy "Miss Granachan", said she "This is the happiest day of my life, I got married this morning" - before Aunty Maggie could reply, young Mary interrupted, tactlessly, (and not a little unmannerly) in surprise "Why Mrs K- I didn't know that J- (the name of the woman's husband) was dead!"

"He isn't" replied the woman, "We have lived together for fifteen years, and only today were we able to get married". "Then I hope you will be very happy", said Aunty Maggie, "You have waited a long time to make things right, and you deserve now to be really happy, the best of luck to you!"

Tears shone in the womans eyes, at the sincerity of the wish, "I knew you'd understand, Miss, that's why I told you about it", and taking up her basket, she went happily on her way.

On another occasion her wealth of sympathy was drawn upon by a poor wizened creature, who sold firewood. She lived in one poorly furnished room always cleanly kept with a sickly husband who was never seen outside his own door. They lived in abject poverty, their only means of livelihood being the firewood that Nellie gathered, and chopped into bundles to sell.

She came one day, again to the kitchen window, the tears falling on to her bundles of wood.

"Why Nellie, what is the matter? you're crying", asked Maggie in consternation, between sobs the poor creature explained that her man had been taken to hospital and was dying, but as they had never been married, she had no claim to see him. It was a sordid story; she had been a prostitute in her young days, and had sunk so low that the magistrates had forbidden her to go within a certain distance of the city centre, under pain of immediate apprehension. She had fallen in love with a young man of good family, and he had forsaken all to live in poverty with her. Then after years of ill health, realising that he was dying, and she could not help him, she had written to his people of their plight. The relatives visited them, and had the sick man removed to hospital, but forbade Nellie to even approach the dying man. After twenty years of hunger and poverty, the struggle for existence only made worth while by the love they had known for each other, the desolate woman was left alone, bereft of the comfort of being with her man in his last agonies.

There was nothing anyone could do to help the woman, but the kindness of Maggie's soothing words healed the aching heart a little, and Nellie went away comforted. No disgust or shrinking from the immoral lives of these poor women did Maggie ever show, only the boundless pity that only a truly great heart can feel. It was no wonder that they came to her with their joy's and sorrows.

Kate and Mary were less tolerant than Maggie, perhaps because they were out in the world more, and as a consequence, liked people less. Mary with her intolerance of any human faults, and Kate with her fiery impatience were not so angelic as Maggie. Of the three perhaps Kate was the most humanly human. She liked a joke and enjoyed going about, sometimes her weakness led her into trouble. She enjoyed a "bottle of stout", and sometimes would call in for one on her way home from work with her companions from the mill. One drink would lead to another, and it must be recorded that Kate had "no head for the drink" while her friends would remain clear eyed and sober, Kate would suddenly become glassy eyed and fuddled, and would arrive home in a state of jubilant intoxication, to the utter disgust of Mary, (who liked her own bottle of stout, but knew when to stop) and the ministrations of Maggie. As these bouts were few and far between, occurring only about once a year, Kate was forgiven by all, her dejected attitude for days after, showing her sorrow for her relapse. Yet these little episodes made her more endearing, they acted as an antidote to Mary's religious hankerings, which though admirable, were thrust upon the other members of the family, who's souls and their salvation worried her considerably.

Meanwhile young Mary pursued the even tenor of her way, attending school and church with diligence, exploring the district with interest. She and her friends often crossed over the tramlines, and the waste ground where the circuses were held, to the ramshackle houses which were used for the manufacture of brandy snap, and the crisp brown cones that were made to hold ice cream. There they would peep in at the door, sniffing the air, which was redolent of cooking sugar and treacle, waiting with watering mouths until one of the bakers would give them a handful of the still warm scraps of brandy snap, or a few of the twists which had been damaged in the making.

Nearby, also was the Italian quarter, and there the children would go, to watch the ice cream being made in the white washed, stone flagged places, watching the great churns turning, and sometimes helping to pour into them the delicious mixture of cornflour, eggs, sugar and milk. One child's mother, sick of her importuning for ice cream from a certain man's cart, had said; "No, you can't have any of that, Mr F- mixes his ice cream with his sweaty feet!"

In vain did the little girl hang around Mr F's ice cream shed, - she didn't ever see him remove his boots, much less mix his ice cream with his feet, although she insisted that once she had found a toe nail in an ice cream sandwich. Which goes to show the faith that children have in the pronouncements of their parents.

The crowds of patient cattle being driven to the slaughter houses behind the markets, sent the children behind them to see if there was any chance of witnessing a killing. The butchers with their bloodstained aprons, and huge axes holding a dreadful attraction for some of the hardier boys, the stench of the abattoir and the sight of the bloodstained floor being enough to make the more squeamish ones turn away.

Sometimes a young bullock would break away from the herd, and go careering along the streets, scattering the people in its path, a horde of laughing children and an angry drover chasing after it. On one occasion a lady behind the counter of a green grocery shop was surprised to see a bullock run in, and make its way towards her. The frightened girl ran up the narrow staircase to the kitchen, the animal in pursuit. The stairs weren't wide enough for it to pass up them, and the beast was imprisoned between the wall and the bannister until the drovers came and tethered it. As the animal could not be persuaded to move either up or down the steps, the bannister had to be removed, and to the relief of the shopkeeper was led away to its inescapable fate.

Soon new activity came to the street where the family lived, breaking up what was left of the calm of the not so peaceful Sabbath. An enterprising sportsman introduced Sunday Boxing Competitions, using a room in an old warehouse, (which had in the older days been used as a school for youthful delinquents, and was often still called the "Ragged School", earned doubtless by the shabby appearance of the pupils who had attended it. Streams of people came to watch these contests, and after the fights had begun, crowds who had not gone inside to watch the bouts, hung around outside craning their necks to see through the windows, and the open doors. Young lads climbed up the drainpipes and swarmed upon the window sills, to have an illicit view, the more daring even sitting on the roof, though what they saw from there of the boxing was a mystery. Anyway, it was as "good an excuse" as any for these urchins to try their skill, and there they sat, their shrill laughter and jokes, adding to the clamour of their alarmed parents, and the roar of the spectators within the building. Those sweltering summer Sundays, when the gas tar bubbled between the cobblestones in the roadways, and the sun beat down upon the shabby naked roof tops, and the people sat outside their tiny houses which resembled miniature "Black Holes of Calcutta", will they never come again? The perfect weather of summertime, I mean, not the conditions it found on such places as the Bank! Now that all the dwellers there have been moved to better housing conditions and have gardens to cultivate and take their leisure in, the weather seems to have gone against them, and those lovely days appear to have vanished with the old slums.

This boxing booth did not last very long but another venturesome sportsman opened another soon afterwards at the lower end of the street which was a success, and was kept open for a long period until it was eventually destroyed by fire, and the promoter took his business further away from the district, and once again a measure of Sabbatarian peace reigned.

# Chapter XI

Mary at fifteen years and a half, suddenly decided that her lifelong ambition of becoming a school teacher was not her dream at all. The Charleston craze was sweeping the country, and ballroom dancing was at the height of its popularity in the city. Mary longed to go to dances, which longing her father opposed on the grounds that she was too young, and that dancing would interfere with her studies. Characteristically Mary disposed of the main objection, by deciding to leave the college and go out to work. In vain did her aunts plead for the years of study which would be wasted. Wasted! Mary laughed, what years spent in happiness could ever be considered as wasted? Those years at school were precious even as memories, and what little knowledge she had gained would come in useful at some time, however remote! So she went to work at the same factory as Kitty, on clerical work, with a promise of a job in the offices if ever a vacancy arose.

Kitty was nearly eighteen now, still not as tall as Mary, her hair had been bobbed and gone was the tiny schoolgirl with the golden plaits, who had started there so shyly long ago. She was an orderseeker now, looking after specially wanted jobs, and her fiery temper added impetus to her always uncontrollable tongue. She took her young sister under her wing, a thing that was scarcely necessary as Mary's placid nature did not leave room for much worry or unhappiness. The knack of settling down where ever she was planted, and just being happy was one that Mary possessed. "In here" she would say "and the place is mine", and sure enough, the surroundings became friendly and Mary was happy. The two sisters, although very fond of each other could never be all in all to each other, Kitty taking life seriously, worrying her head over trifles, Mary being happy go lucky and not worrying at all over anything.

In money matters too the sisters were different. However much Kitty spent of her slender means, she could always produce a few shillings from somewhere. Mary never seemed to have any money, often giving her last twopence to a beggar in the street, declaring that when she was broke she was happiest. Edward had started to "keep company" with a young lady, and they were both enthusiastic dancers, but round about this time, a new sport had taken the fancy of the public, and John had started to make a book at the greyhound racing track which had opened in the city, and Edward went along there to work for his father.

So the wily Mary had her way about going to dances, for was not Edward's young lady able to teach them, and take care of them? That was the beginning of their going to dances, for John could not object when his future daughter in-law offered to take the young girls with her, and keep them out of mischief. Often John would come to meet them, standing outside the dancehall door as they came out, just like, as Mary remarked, the heavy father in some Victorian novel.

Then one night, perched upon her father's knee Mary tackled him on the subject "Dad", she asked "Don't you trust us?"

"What ever do you mean?" asked John in surprise. "Well, you come along to meet us from dances, or sit waiting up for us when we come home. After a lovely evening the pleasure is all gone, when you start asking us, which way did we come home? who was with us? How long did we take to get home, - almost as though you had a stop watch in your hand!"

"It isn't that I don't trust you dear, but I worry about you, so young to be out late at night, and you may get mixed up with bad characters in the dance halls"

"Now dad, we go to dance, and not get mixed up with bad characters. There are always a few girls come home together so no one will molest us. We feel so silly when you come to meet us as though we were babies".

"You are babies to me", replied John, "and I'm afraid of your meeting with any drunken men on your way home".

"No drunken man could run as fast as we can" said Mary " so there's nothing whatever for you to worry about. We will take care of ourselves, and be careful of the company we keep and promise never to do anything of which you wouldn't approve, so please dad, don't come to meet us anymore".

John didn't trouble the girls again, and a new understanding sprang up between him and his youngest child as a result of their talk together.

The aunts weren't too happy about the frequent dances the girls attended, their fear that it might impair the health of their nieces worrying them not a little, but the bloom of health still remained on the rosy cheeks they had watched over from babyhood, so their anxiety grew less. They loved to watch the girls put on their dance dresses and go out with sparkling eyes, and would wait up to hear an account of the evening's enjoyment. For all these jolly times spent outside the district, the girls still attended the socials and dances given at the church hall, so their lives were full indeed.

Then came their first seaside holiday away from their aunts, and the household was in a ferment of excitement. New dresses to be made, odds and ends to get together put new life into the aunts, as they threw themselves wholeheartedly into the joyful anticipation of the girls. Edward's young lady - Mollie, made all the dresses, and they were a pleasure to behold. She was also going with them, along with a friend of hers. At last the time came to catch the train, and with everything packed, the aunts asked how the girls, who had been saving up for this holiday, were placed financially. Kitty produced several pound notes which she had drawn from a holiday fund she had contributed to, - enough to pay for everything and to have plenty left. Mary produced an amount which, with the price of her railway ticket deducted, left her with exactly twenty five shillings! - and this to cover her 'digs' and other expenses. There was a prompt collection amongst the three aunts and Mary went away with a well filled purse.

This disregard of money often showed in Mary's adventures. She would arrange to go off to the country or seaside for a day with friends and when all ready to set out would suddenly remember that she possessed about a shilling at the most, and a hasty hint had to be given to her father to supply the needed cash. Pehaps if she had had to rely on her own resources her sense of money would have been differently developed.

Their first holiday in Blackpool was a round of enjoyment, and to the young girls it was a second heaven, marred only by the sunburn incurred, which was a painful experience that marred an otherwise perfect week, and they returned home full of life and spirits, to their aunts, who had been lonely without them.

As time went on the children, who had not had a lot of interest in their Aunt Mary, found her to be the most broadminded of their aunts. Aunt Kate still held their hearts as the one with whom they could share a joke, but she was very severe in her ciriticisms of the rising generations, although sometimes her views were contradictions. She encouraged the girls to have their hair waved and curled, although still deploring the loss of their long plaits. Of their dresses she was a keen critic, and one had to be well groomed indeed to pass her eagle eye. She approved of make up on anyone who needed a touch of cosmetic improvement, but hated the thought of her nieces using the dusting of powder which was the only make up they needed with their fresh complexions. Of women smoking, she had an absolute horror, and used strong language on the subject when she found cigarettes in Mary's handbag.

When Mary protested that there was nothing indecent in a woman smoking, Aunt Kate was almost speechless, and Aunt Maggie took up the cudgels on her behalf. "Perhaps when I tell you that Father M- told me that most of the girls in Dublin smoke, even on the buses and tramcars", said the wily Mary - speaking truthfully, "And that he and the other priests have offered their cigarettes to the ladies on trips and at socials, you will agree that there is no harm in the practice".

The bubble of the aunt's indignation was burst, for what was good enough for Dublin was all right with Maggie, and Kate could not go on in the face of such a declaration, but still she always sniffed disgustedly, and went into an exaggerated fit of coughing whenever she came across her niece enjoying a cigarette.

Kitty missed the general disapproval in this respect, as cigarettes did not appeal to her, after her first attempt at smoking, which left her choking for breath and with streaming eyes. She preferred to eat chocolates and sweets, which she bought very often. Sometimes in the middle of the week, when Mary was as usual, without money, Kitty would suggest going to the cinema in town, often with one of their girl friends, Kitty buying a couple of bags of sweets, and paying for Mary's ticket into the picture house.

On the way thither, Kitty would keep on worrying, - the place would be full, but they must try to get three seats together. On no account must they be separated. She always gave the other two girls the sweets to carry, as she disliked bulging pockets, and they would not fit in her handbag. On getting inside the darkened cinema, the three would grope their way up the aisle following the usherette. Suddenly Kitty would spy a single seat, and fearful that they wouldn't find another would dive into the row and take it. The other two would go further along and often find a row with several seats empty. There they would sit enjoying the picture and Kitty's sweets, until the show was over, and they all met again. This happened several times until it became a standing joke, every time Kitty insisted that they got three seats together, but her worrying nature would not let her wait for them to materialise!

On another occasion they were standing in a picture queue waiting for the cheaper seats, when the doorman called out that there was no waiting for seats at a dearer price. Kitty rushed out of the queue, leaving her companions, and paid the extra money. Five minutes later the picture house emptied considerably, and the patient queue was let inside. Imagine Kitty's chagrin when

Mary and her friends walked in and calmly sat down beside her having paid the cheaper rates!

Perhaps, of the two sisters, Kitty was more lovable, for her nature made her take everyone elses troubles to heart. As Mary often remarked "Kitty is never happy unless she has something to worry about", and there is no one so well liked by any other human being than the person who feels and shares their troubles. Mary's more philosophical nature saw the funny side of most tragic things, even if she sympathised with them, and her levity Kitty labelled as "callous". Yet even Mary's levity or calloussness healed many a wound that would have festered with too much sympathy, and the practical views she held were often sought and accepted by their mutusal friends and acquaintances.

The sisters had a great friend, a petite dark haired, brown eyed girl whom, as no one cared much for her name, which was Ethel, they renamed "Babs", as her one regret was that she had not been christened Barbara. One evening they were at a dance, and as there were few partners available, Babs asked Mary to dance with her. They danced together very well, but as Mary was much taller than her friend, she felt a trifle uncomfortable. Again they danced together, but on Babs' third request Mary refused, pointing out the difference in their respective heights, "We look like Mutt and Jeff" she remarked. Babs was extremely annoyed at this sally, and sulked for a greater part of the night, until Mary finally approached her "Babs", she demanded "Do you want to be a friend of mine or not?" "Why of course I do" answered the surprised Babs. "Then for heavens sake, stop sulking, as I don't allow anyone of that nature to be a friend of mine. I say what I think is true, and expect you to tell me if you don't approve, and not sit in a corner and sulk about it" Suddenly

Babs smiled, "All right Mary, I should have known better - I'll never sulk again!" and she never did, - often repeating the story with great zest.

After working with Kitty for about six months, Mary got a job at one of the largest clothing firms in the city. The girls with whom she worked were mostly from the outlying country districts, and went out five minutes before the usual dinner time to "mash teas" - the Yorkshire equivalent for the brewing of tea. They told Mary that they got a free dinner for doing this, and Mary, greenhorn as she was, thought that it was a fine organisation which gave free dinners to the girls who troubled to make their own tea. On a certain day, one of these girls was away ill, and the others asked Mary if she would take her place, so Mary found herself leaving early with the others to go down into the canteen. They marched behind the counter, and a huge enamel jug was put into Mary's hand, and she was told to fill it with boiling water from the geyser. Suddenly the awful truth dawned on her. She was to stand at the counter to fill the mugs which were put upon it by the queues of workpeople, and pour it over their "mashings" of tea or cocoa which they had brought from home. Scarlet faced with the steamy heat and embarrassment, the heavy jug awkward in her unaccustomed hands, she stood there filling up the mugs for her hundreds of fellow workers, clumsily slopping the water over the tops of the pots, or only half filling some in her anxiety not to overflow them too, her feet splashed with the boiling water and her overall wet through. The crowning moment came when they went for the free dinner, which happened to be Mary's favourite one of roast pork, seasoning and apple sauce, only to find that there were only potatoes and gravy and a small portion of meat left, and the pudding which she preferred was gone too.   Never again could she be persuaded to go along and "mash the teas"!

# Chapter XII

The day of Edward's marriage dawned, after much feverish activity on the part of Mollie and the girls, who were to be bridesmaids. It was a day to be remembered by those guests who were invited, and the hundred odd others who found their way there in the evening, for a dance was held after the wedding feast, and the drinks were abundant.

It was hard to believe that such an irresponsible fellow was at last going to settle down, and the aunts and John were feeling happy about it. Edward had caused them more anxiety than the other two children, his escapades giving them many heart burnings. Perhaps he was unlucky, who can say, but in any mischief, he was always the one caught out. He was headstrong and had a curious sense of humour, as when he was racing his motorbike along a road, and a fellow tried to cross it. "It was a race between him and I" said Eddie later, describing the incident, "And we made it a dead heat". That there wasn't a dead pedestrian was fortunate for Edward; it was John had to go along, and visit the injured man and pay him compensation for his loss of work owing to the accident.

On another occasion, Edward was driving a car in Scotland, when going over a hump backed bridge he went dangerously near a young couple who were walking along it. After an altercation between him and the irate young man, who insisted that his young lady's life had been endangered, a charge of dangerous driving was made against Edward, and when he came back home, a summons awaited him, calling him to return to Scotland. He did so, and after answering the charge, on the way home he rode through a flock of sheep, scaring them and the shepherd out of their wits. He spent the night in the local police station, and after a good lecture and a caution, he was sent on his way.

These and sundry other escapades kept his aunts in a state of trepidation when ever he went out, especially as once he rode his motorbike for half a mile before he discovered that Mollie had fallen off the pillion, owing to the jolting of the cobbled roads, and they lived in dread of worse accidents befalling them. Now that the motorcycle was sold, and matrimony was imminent, the aunts breathed a trifle more freely.

At this time John had taken an office in the city centre, and was a licenced commission agent, and was doing fairly well in the business. Aunty Kate was not working, as the mill she had worked in had closed down in the slump, so she stayed home and helped Maggie with the housework, but Mary still went out to her mill work every day. Although the children had grown up and were well able to look after themselves, Maggie still could not be persuaded to go out any where, either to the theatre or cinemas, or any church functions. The only time she went outdoors was to slip out to early mass on Sundays and holidays when the family were still abed, and to do her shopping. Perhaps it was the old shyness from which she had never recovered, or maybe that she had got so accustomed to staying at home that she found no reason strong enough for her to leave it.

There was always some one coming and going to and from the house, John's associates and the girls' companions, but they seldom saw Maggie, as she always kept herself in the background, yet these young girls all knew and loved her, struck by the gentle quality and sweetness they recognised on the rare occasions they saw her. To most of them she was Aunty Maggie too.

When Edward's first child was born, the aunts were overjoyed and looked forward to the time when the little one could come to them, for were not all children welcome at their house, and a grand niece would be doubly dear.

It took John a considerable time to realise that he was a grandfather, as the years had passed so swiftly that he still imagined that his own daughters were still babies. On one occasion, he and a friend who had spent a convivial evening together, called into the fish and chip shop to bring something home for supper. He recognised a young lady, who had played with Kitty and Mary as children, but was now engaged to be married, "Here Charlie" said John , "I want you to meet Miss "So and So" - she plays with my kiddies!" His "kiddies" at that particular moment, were having the time of their lives at the town hall dance!

The years had been kind to John, he was still the handsome athletic person of his youthful days, and his early training, coupled with his open air life, plenty of exercise and turkish baths, kept his muscles as firm and pliable as they had been long ago. Sometimes he would irritate his daughters by striding swiftly up and down the passages and running up a flight of steps, then down again, continuously for hours at a time. "What ever is the matter dad?" they would ask "Why all this prowling around?"

"I'm taking my exercise", John would reply "Then for goodness sake, why not go out for a long walk or something?" was the irritable query "Because I've taken some opening medicine, and I don't want to go far away" would come the naive reply, and the brisk promenading would recommence.

He would sit for hours "studying form" race cards and turf guides piled up around him, glaring at any interruption of his work. "Hush!" the girls would say, with flippant irreverence - "Dad is reading his bible!", and the aunts would smile, although a little scandalised, and would keep as quiet as possible. As Mary often remarked what good all this "studying form" did she couldn't imagine, as John seemed to back less winners than anyone else in the racing world, but Maggie would smile tolerantly and say "It doesn't do any harm though, it keeps him quiet and occupied".

John often took Kitty and Mary to the theatre to see any good shows that were on, and every week took them to the pictures in town, he was a good host, and when the girls were with him, he was as gallant and courteous to them as any beau could have been. On these occasions, he gave Mary one cigarette, calling it her rations, as he did not really approve of young ladies smoking. On one of these occasions he forgot to give Mary her "ration", and she restlessly signalled to Kitty, who famous for her tactless remarks, said to her father, "Dad, give Mary a cigarette, she's gasping for a smoke", "Gasping for a smoke!" growled John, "I'll take her outside and spank her behind in a minute!", but his sense of humour overcame him, and he offered Mary the long awaited cigarette.

If John had taken care of his money, and had he had any business sense, he could have been a fairly rich man, but his generous nature, coupled with the disregard for money that Mary had inherited, kept his wealth at a minimum. Often when the girls were with him, some needy man would stop him, and they would see a note slipped surreptitiously into the other man's palm. On occasions when John was short of cash he would catch a tram into town, only five minutes walk away, explaining that it saved him at least ten shillings, as there was always someone who needed help, on the way to town, and he couldn't afford to give anything that day. Strict, yet soft hearted, military yet inefficient, that was the father the girls so dearly loved.

Aunty Mary, still working in the mill had a terrible accident. Her hand got caught in one of the big machines, and it was crushed, the huge steel pins in the machine tearing the flesh to ribbons. The specialists at the infirmary shook their heads when they saw it, and declared that the hand should be amputated. Mary stood firm, however, declaring that if they could do anything with it, she would stand any pain, if only she could keep her hand. The doctors decided to do their best, and put the mutilated hand under treatment. Luckily, the guiders of the hand were not broken, so there was a chance that the hand could be saved. The sight of the bare bones, stripped of their flesh, which clustered in lumps at the finger tips, looking like a skeleton hand which had been dipped amongst crushed strawberries, made the younger Mary weep uncontrollably, - she who was so hard where tragedy was concerned. The fortitude of the injured woman was magnificent, and she was never heard to cry out or even give any sign of pain, when every half hour the injured limb had to be thrust into hot water. What she suffered, no one will ever know, but the white hairs that came into the dark head told their own story. After months of treatment, the hand began to heal, and through sheer will power, Mary made it move again. The useless fingers were massaged and with great patience, she could grasp small objects. Never again could Mary return to the mills, but she thanked God, who had spared her hand, and made it useful again.

So now the three sisters were all at home and life was not as peaceful as before, for what three women could live closely confined together, and not have any differences of opinion? Kate's hasty temper and Mary's contrariness kept poor Maggie in the role of peacemaker, until, by common consent, the two elder sisters solved the problem. They seldom stayed in the same room together, one rising to leave the room as the other entered, their nieces finding this a very entertaining state of affairs. Kate had only to disapprove of any project of her nieces to bring Mary ranging at their side, or vice versa Maggie tried hard to keep the balance of power, but sometimes it tried even her vast patience.

In one thing though, the whole household agreed unanimously, and that was the fuss they made of Margaret, Edward's little girl, and the baby brother who followed her into the world fifteen months later. Their greatest joy was when the children came to visit them every Sunday, and there was nothing they would not do to make the babies happy.

When Kitty and Mary went to Ireland for a holiday Aunty Maggie went back to the days of her youth, and could never hear enough of the things they had seen there. As they had only spent a week in Wicklow, they hadn't seen very much of the Ireland she had loved to hear about from her mother's lips, yet, they had been to her dreamland, and that was all that mattered. News had come from a friend who had visited the old home of her mother, that a few of the old relations were still alive there, and set new longing in Maggie's heart, for the country her mother had loved. In imagination she visited the old spots, but could not be persuaded to make the journey in reality. Perhaps someday, she will pluck up the courage, and go there, if so she will be the happiest woman alive, but I am convinced that if she is ever called to another world before she visits Ireland, St Peter, standing at the golden gate, will bring St Patrick to meet her, for are not heaven and Ireland almost synonymous to her? The silver, gold and darker threads that go into the weaving of life's pattern were nowhere more apparent than in the tapestry of the "Ham Shank". There was always the golden thread of humour to lighten the blackest hours, and the sombre shades to contrast with the shining light of faith that shone in the hearts of some of the dwellers there.

The tall kindly Bishop in his top hat, that gleamed with a silken sheen, often walked slowly up the streets, stopping to pat the heads of the children as they left their play to run to him for one of his kindly words, giving his blessing to the shabby people, or the well clad ones, who knelt to kiss the great ruby in his episcopal ring, was a common enough sight in that place of contradictions, where a Bishop could walk in peace, but policemen were always seen in pairs.

One of the children who lived in abject poverty dreamed wonderful dreams and told the other children at school of her beautiful home, and brought the sceptical ones along to see her golden piano and the lovely drawing room. On reaching the humble dwelling she left her companions and went inside, only to return in a moment to say that her father was sitting in the drawing room, "He sits there all day long", she explained, "What does he sit there all day long for, what does he do?" asked one of the children "Why, he draws you silly - what else is a drawing room for?" said the dreamer. As the only thing the father would draw with any pleasure was a pint of old and mild, there was pathos as well as humour in the story.

There was the kindly, humble priest, who still wore the shabby hat he had rescued from the dustbin of a seminary, years before on seeing one of the students throw it away. He was a very erudite man, a Professor of Theology and a great authority on Greek, yet his simple kindliness endeared everyone to him, whether learned or otherwise, and with an unusual taste in literature for such an intellect as he possessed. He liked any kind of detective fiction, and was happy when a parcel of these books were sent to him, along with the sweets and chocolate that he distributed amongst the children.

Amongst the darker threads there was the "blind"' man, who begged in the city, complete with dark glasses, tapping stick and canine guide, who of an evening was to be seen sitting in his house perusing the sporting pink, the study of which seemed quite profitable if one counted the times he went tapping his way to the bookies at paying out time. There was also the one legged man who was the terror of the district, when he got drunk and went berserk. It took half a dozen policemen to catch him, when he was driven into a corner and, with his back against the wall, he took off his wooden leg and used it as a club, cracking any crown that came within radius.

There was the very old man who was seen daily taking his slow feeble walk. On one occasion the rumour went abroad that he had died. On his next appearance, a bewildered man looked at him in surprise "Why Mr K-" he exclaimed, "I heard you were dead", "Oh I'm not dead", came the dry reply "They just buried me 'on spec'!"

One fat blousy woman, with a great mottled face and eyes that continually watered with "beery tears" bore the name of

Josephine. She was loud, she was vulgar, but good humour emanated from her. Night after night she spent in her favourite public house, keeping up a friendly feud with the landlord, who was just as small as she was huge. When closing time came, the diminutive landlord pretended to be tough, and tried to throw the big woman out. Eventually they would reach the street. Josephine with her face shining like a big red sun. "Get along you little short assed b-", she would say "You're all right shutting the door on us when you can't sell us any more beer!" "Now then Jos. there's many a big potato rotten! Good stuff lies in little room!" the little man would tease her, and then the air would be filled with a volley of oaths worthy of any sergeant major. After a few minutes of these profane, if comical passages, the woman would move along "Good night and God Bless you" she would cry and the landlord would return the salutation. Broad was their speech, and coarse their humour, yet there was still the remembrance of better lives lived in their youth in that last "Good night and God Bless".

Amongst the more neutral shades the people who spent their lives working hard, spending their leisure in simple pleasure, were the background of the picture, people whose quiet existence gave out no high lights, their quiet joys and silent sorrows raising no fantastic design on the tapestry of life. Unnoticed they went their way, their uneventful lives important only to themselves, eating, sleeping, working and resting, most of their days so like the others that weeks passed into years, only the maturing of their children bringing to their notice the passage of time.

Perhaps because of the rather haphazard way in which John earned his living, Edward now working for him, the lives of the Granachan family differed slightly from that of their neighbours.

The regular working hours of the girls gave Maggie little worry as to their meal times, but John was most irregular in his habits, rushing in at any time for a meal, always in the same tearing hurry. Although he didn't do much travelling to racecourses, there was still the old excuse of "a fellow to meet at such a time - I'm late already" to send Maggie scurrying about the kitchen. In all the years she had looked after the house, John's rushing ways could still unnerve her. It was useless for her nieces to laughingly protest that their father was always late for something, and that she mustn't get excited about it, the mere appearance of John seemed to make Maggie flutter around like a frightened bird. The other sisters worried about John too, for he was a born gambler, and often spent half the night at some club or other in town, arriving home with the dawn, uncertain of gait and often the lighter in pocket. On some occasions the noise of a taxi would bring the sisters from their uneasy slumbers, and John would arrive, trying to quieten the noise of the friends who were still in the cab, creeping into the house like a naughty school boy caught out on some mischievous prank.

The frequenting of these clubs, at which John had won (and lost again) so much money, gave Edward an idea. Why not start a club of their own? There would be only the necessary number of members applications to be procured, the licence got, and hey-presto, their fortune would be made! It was remarkable, that Edward could always see the easy way to make a fortune, yet he was still in the same position, year after year. His powers of persuasion however, were greater than his ability to amass wealth, and John agreed to turn the office into a social club, and they launched forth on their new project with high hopes, and more new fears for the aunts, and heart burnings for Kitty. Mary didn't care much either way as she maintained, John would find a way to be parted from his money anyhow, so it may as well be in his own club as any one else's.

The night life, with its heavy drinking and smokefilled atmosphere made very little difference to John, thanks to his marvellous physique, but its laid its mark upon Edward in no uncertain manner. Gone were the tanned cheeks of other days, and his never overlarge frame seemed to shrink. He drank too much and in drink was not the most congenial of companions. His humour took on a bitter scoffing quality, and he was often in trouble because of his offensive sallies.

This worried the aunts a great deal, for they shrank from scenes, and hated the thought that Edward was the cause of some rather unpleasant ones. They disliked the new mode of life their brother had undertaken, knowing that the gambling at the club and the drinking after hours was illegal, and that the hand of the law would fall heavily upon them. The fact that the city had several of these places, which were periodically raided, and closed, then opened out again on other premises, failed to give any comfort to their worrying hearts. All they could do was pray that no harm would befall their brother and his son.

Kitty was still working at the same factory, but her health was not too good. She fainted, periodically, but would never stay away from work a day if she could any way avoid it. Mary was still dancing her way through the evenings, work to her being a nuisance that made early rising imperative. Work she didn't mind in the least, as she was happy in her jobs, but having to rise from a warm comfortable bed made her groan in spirit, and seldom was she early on the premises. How she didn't get the

sack for unpunctuality was a thing that her father never could discover.

At one place she worked at, the firm started work at eight o'clock, and any late comers up to half past eight or nine were made to wait the manager's displeasure, often kept there for half an hour cooling their heels to wait for a lecture from him. On several occasions Mary walked past the manager whilst he was delivering these lectures, giving him a polite and smiling good-morning, which he returned, never dreaming that anyone would dare to come in so late. She never earned any wages worth talking about, but was happy in spite of little money, as whenever she needed anything badly, her father or aunts supplied the necessary cash.

Country life appealed to Mary and there she spent every week end, tramping the fields, and green hedged lanes, sleeping in an old caravan that she and her friends had rented, living free and easy lives, full of health and spirits. The long walk to mass on Sundays made them early risers as the nearest church was three miles away, and often they went to one six miles away, but the sight of the dew drenched grass, and the pure morning air made early rising a pleasure, even for the lazy Mary.

John was still in the club, and doing well, although his sisters were not reconciled to the idea yet, and went in constant fear of his getting into trouble. Also a gang of toughs and such like, who fancied themselves as strong armed men, were frequenting such places, and provoking quarrels which gave them the opportunity for a free for all fight. One night, the ringleader of this gang came with his brother to John's place, and after drinking more than enough he was refused any more liquor. He started a violent argument with Edward, but John interposed and taking the man in hand, threw him out, nursing a badly bruised jaw. A couple of nights later, the whole gang descended like wolves on the fold, but this time the "lambs" were prepared. John, still as fit as a fiddle, although now around fifty four, tackled the leader who had some reputation as a boxer, and gave him a thorough thrashing. Edward, though not so strong was game, and the men who worked for them took on the rest. In a short while, the pugnacious crowd found themselves being thrown down the steps outside the club, with the victory in the hands of John and his friends.

A few days later Edward was walking along one of the town's main streets when he saw, coming towards him, the leader of the "tough guys". With all the goodwill of the victor towards the vanquished, Edward advanced with hand outstretched "Hello B-" said he. The other man made a movement as though to shake hands with the unsuspecting Edward, then with a swift upward movement, plucked the spectacles from Edward's nose, gave him a terrific punch between the eyes and replaced the spectacles. He strode away, leaving poor Edward sitting on the pavement, counting the stars which were bursting around him! Afterwards in telling the story, he said, That he didn't mind the blow so much, but the business of removing his glasses was adding insult to injury.

# Chapter XIV

About this time, there was a stir of housebuilding by the city council. At last, slums had come to be recognised as such, and areas were taken over by the council, and new housing estates were built, to replace the old and worn out houses of the slums. Mary had turned sixty years of age, and, although she still had the same erect carriage, her hair was almost white, and her once keen eyesight was already dim. The Catholic religion was her first thought, and almost her only outdoor excursions were to church. Neither hail nor snow would prevent her, and indeed today, at the age of seventy four, she has only been known to miss mass on Sunday once, as the snow was very deep and the way too treacherous in that weather for a person of her age. Kate had not altered greatly, her weight was considerably reduced, although she would never recover the sylph like figure of her youth, and the injured foot still made her walk slowly and heavily.

To her nieces at least, Maggie was the least altered of the three aunts. Her hair was still dark and smooth, the grey which had crept into the hair of Mary and Kate had not as yet touched hers. The three sisters lived quietly, seldom leaving the house, although Maggie often declared that she had always detested the place, but could not be prevailed upon to go anywhere else. The news of the slum clearance scheme was much discussed by the three sisters, indeed it soon grew to be the sole, or almost so, topic of conversation in the district, many stories, funny and otherwise were told by the gossiping people. One of the ladies on the housing committee, came round to inspect the goods and chattels of the families who were on the list for immediate removal. She strolled through the houses with a curt and supercilious air, telling the people what things they could take into their new houses and the things that must be destroyed. A verminous house had to be decontaminated with a poisonous gas, before the furniture and other things could be removed. This was not a success, as the people often hid things in neighbour's houses that they thought would be spoiled by the gas, taking them later on to their new houses. Also, the stoving process, although killing a lot of the vermin, drove the rest through the old walls into the houses of people who had kept them clean and free from such pests.

On one occasion it was told of this officious lady, (whether true or not I can't say) that she went into one house and prodded a mattress with her pencil, to see if there was any "live stock" thriving in it. A moment later, she put the pencil up, in a characteristic gesture to tap her cheek with it. To her horror, and the householder's amusement, a bug ran down the pencil on to the petrified lady's face!

So a new system was instituted, a decontamination van, in which every one's household goods, whether they were clean or otherwise were removed, the gas being let into the vans and left there for several hours. This fair system was more liked, as it gave less embarrassment to the people who had worked to keep their houses clean, and at the last were getting the vermin and dirt of their less particular neighbours, and soon the "bug van'" as it was facetiously called was a frequent visitor to the district.

At first the loss of people and the empty houses were not noticeable, but soon whole streets were emptied, the gaping holes where the doors and windows had been, and the broken fireplaces testifying to the industry of certain enterprising men who sold the old wood and glass, and the firegrates and irons for a good price to the salvage merchants of the town. Soon the council realised the value of such stuff and sent their own men to collect them, but as most of the old wood wasn't fit for use, it was burnt by them, in huge bonfires that delighted the hearts of the younger members of the community.

It was the large families living in overcrowded quarters that were given preference, and the more delapidated of the old courts and yards of the district. They went in high hopes; the new houses with their baths and modern equipment were a boon to the housewife who had to wash, cook and do all her work in one room, hindered by the rest of the family who had no other place to sit unless they spent their leisure hours in the bedrooms, or bedroom - for often there was only one living and one bedroom in the houses. The old people were pathetic, torn from the place in which they had spent their lives, however poor and humble. They were bewildered at the change in their circumstances. The flats they were given (to rent) were compact and neat, with laboursaving devices, but the hearts of the old folk were amongst the tumble down dwellings where flitted the ghosts of their past joys and sorrows, where they had heard the first wailing cries of their children, or kissed the cold lips of loved ones whom they would never meet again in life.

Yes, indeed, the Bank presented a strange sight now, with its rows of dead and broken houses, the lampstandards casting a fitful radiance on their sightless windows. The bands of starving cats, their eyes gleaming out of the blackness, snarling and fighting together over some piece of offal that had been discovered, or mewing piteously for warmth and comfort near the houses that were still inhabited.

During the hectic period when the people were moving away, Maggie had a bad accident. She fell down the stone steps leading to the kitchen and broke her leg. On hearing the noise of the fall Kitty and Mary ran to her rescue, the ashen colour of her face and the black rings of pain under her eyes telling of the great pain she was enduring. For the first time in her life she was compelled to stay in bed or rather, on a settee, as she was unable to go upstairs, and do nothing. Owing to her foolish prejudice against doctors, which really amounted to her inordinate shyness, she refused medical help until the pain forced her to give in. Mary had tended the swollen foot, and bandaged it, and when the doctor came and arranged for an x-ray photograph, it showed that one of the small foot bones had been broken, but had joined together again. As the specialist explained, if he broke the bone again and re-set it, the new joint would probably not be as good as the one Mary had so accidently made, so they decided to leave it alone, and precribe a surgical boot and calipers to help Maggie walk again.

This seemed to be the beginning of a run of ill luck, John also broke his wrist, - as Edward described the accident, two dogs were fighting on the pavement, and John - "always a gentleman" - stepped off the curb to give them plenty of room, and slipped, fracturing his wrist in the fall,!, so there were two people in the household with broken bones. John soon recovered the use of his hand, but Maggie was doomed to limp for the rest of her life.

It was no longer the same lively street they had known. Most of the houses were empty, and the green blades of grass were pushing their way through the cobbles in the empty side streets. When the girls went out at night, the dark, deserted streets with only a lighted window here and there, took on a sinister appearance they had never worn even in the old hectic days when the "Ham Shank" was notorious for the rogues and toughs who made it their headquarters. Homeless vagrants made their lodgings for the night in the more weatherproof of the derelict houses, giving nervous qualms to those people who still lived around, and had never known fear of the district and its inhabitants before.

If the girls went to any of the dances at the church, they had to go through the rows of deserted streets, and the midnight walks home were not too pleasant. Often if they saw a policeman on his solitary beat they would keep him company until within sight of their own house. The obliging officer would shine his lamp down the street, a friendly beacon, until they were safely at their own gate, and called out to him a friendly "goodnight and thank you".

When the news came that they were to get a new house, they were all excited, and the girls went to inspect it and pronounce judgement on it. It was a good house and they were pleased with it. The aunts were glad too, but sorry to leave the place in which they had lived so long. John also, took a sentimental view of the matter, but Mary and Kitty looked forward to their new surroundings.

The parish of Mount St Mary's had decreased enormously, for two thirds and more of their parishioners had been given new homes in this vast slum clearance scheme, and leaving the church of their childhood was perhaps the only pang that smote the hearts of the younger sisters. The tears and sighs of their aunts too, were mostly for the church they had loved, and they all spoke of the day, when, all the slums cleared away, a new lot of houses would be built and then maybe they could return to their home parish.

What memories must have filled their hearts when at last the day arrived when they were to go into their new home. With the walls denuded of its pictures, and the furniture all stacked in readiness for the removal men, they stood, silent and disconsolate, gazing with fond and tearful eyes at the already unfamiliar look of the house, looking forlorn and deserted now that its trappings had vanished. John wandered around repeating to himself, "Forty three years in one house, its hard to leave it!" "Come along dad, you spent forty years too long in it then!" - this from the indifferent seeming Mary - who nevertheless felt the parting keenly. The men soon had the household goods packed into the "bug van" and they were left in the empty shell of their home, to turn their backs on the old life, and start again on the new.

That new life for them was still hidden by the dark veil of the future, but their memories of the past would always hold sway within the hearts that had beat so long in the turmoil of the busy streets of old "Ham Shank", and always there would be a sweet nostalgic longing for the days that were dead and gone. John would remember his golden haired Rosie, with her babies in her arms, Kate the bonny children who had romped and played with her so long ago. Mary the children she had loved, the sweet sister she had lost, Maggie the days of care and love she had bestowed upon her ailing mother, and the children who had come, motherless to the house that welcomed them. The children would always still be children when they remembered the warmth of love they had received from their aunts, and the games they had played with their companions years ago - of the "beck" with its stinking dirty waters. Of the people they had seen and known in all the glory of their goodness, or those seemingly stripped of all virtues.

The "Ham Shank" now, what memories did it hold of the people who had lived and laughed, loved and quarrelled in its crowded streets. It could have told many a juicy tale, but now its voice is silent, a large tract of land overgrown with coarse grass and weeds, the cobbles almost obliterated, the bricks and mortar that were once homes, vanished completely. Only a few old buildings remain, the cheerless mills divided up into small factories, and the few public houses that still remain, stand bleakly alone, missing the almost throttling embrace of the shabby houses that once leaned against them.

Yet up there on the hill top, gazing serenely at the desolate scene, stands the unchanged church, waiting for the children who were torn away, symbol of the faith that stands enduring when everything else in life has gone its unstable way, knowing that from the old evil dwellings, new ones will arise, clean and wholesome, giving the new generations a chance of more happy and healthy lives.

Still the memory of the old "Ham Shank" will be a pleasant one for one person at least, for there she spent a happy life, under the care of that little brown haired child, who became her best beloved Aunty Maggie, and if only for the characteristic patience and humility of this same aunt, to the writer at least, the Ham Shank justified its existence.

1946